BARATTI AND
ARCHAEOLO(

CW01082112

Editorial Lay-out
Giovanni Breschi,
Silvia Guideri (Parchi Val di Cornia S.p.A.)

Edited by
Silvia Guideri

Texts by
Andrea Semplici

Tessa Matteini, author of scientific box
texts

Texts written by Gianfranco Barsotti and
Antonio Borzatti for the Società Parchi Val
di Cornia have been adapted for the guide
for the chapters entitled "Evolution of the
territory," "Geology," "Landscape and
Vegetation" and "Fauna."
The profiles in "Park Plants" are from the
panels inside the Park and written by
Gianfranco Barsotti and Antonio Borzatti.

Under the scientific direction of Antonella
Romualdi, the scientific texts bear in mind
the historic notes appearing on panels at
the Park Visitors Center's exhibition,
"The Etruscans in Populonia."

Photographs:
Archivio Comune di Piombino
Archivio Società Parchi Val di Cornia
Giovanni Breschi
Soprintendenza Archeologica della Toscana
Enrico Tovoli
Jong Kwon Kim Rigatti

The illustrations and cartography on pages
22 and 23 were taken from panels at the
Baratti and Populonia Archaeological Park
Visitors Center exhibition and made by:
panel design, Paolo Donati and Studio
Inklink; *illustrations,* Studio Inklink
(Simone Boni, Alessandro Rabatti,
Lorenzo Pieri, Luigi Critone, Francesco
Petracchi, Lucia Mattioli); *cartography,*
Alessandro Bartolozzi

Cartography on page 89 is by Sergio Biagi

Graphic lay-out and make-up,
Giovanni Breschi

Translations
Victor Palchetti Beard

© 2002 Edizioni Polistampa
   Sede legale: Via Santa Maria, 27/r - 50125 Firenze
   Tel. 055.233.7702 - Fax 055.229.430
   Stabilimento: Via Livorno, 8/31 - 50142 Firenze
   Tel. 055.7326.272 - Fax 055.7377.428
   http://www.polistampa.com

ISBN 88-8304-460-6

I Parchi della
VAL di CORNIA
from hills to sea from nature to man

Baratti and Populonia
Archaeological Park

Itineraries
to get acquainted
with the territory

Andrea Semplici

℘

EDIZIONI POLISTAMPA

The promontory of Populonia and the gulf of Baratti are today one of the most characteristic landscapes of the Tuscan coast. Rolling hills, Mediterranean underbrush on steep slopes that drop sheer into the blue sea, history and archaeology, all come together to evoke pictorial images. Here, we encounter traces of ancient populations, starting from the beach of Baratti: an open-air museum shining with iron scoria that testifies to the impressiveness of the Etruscan industrial city of Populonia.

From here, climbing up past the necropolises of San Cerbone and Le Grotte, we reach the acropolis of the Etruscan city and the medieval village of Populonia, led by archaeological artifacts narrating millennia of history.

Quite a different fate could have awaited these places if, in the sixties, an attempt was not thwarted to lot the gulf of Baratti and the entire promontory of Populonia, archaeological areas included.

The 1967 Town Development Plan adopted by the municipal administration provided for just short of two million cubic meters of cement in the form of hotels, villages and villas, on these territories. The Ministry of Public Works, however, severed these provisions in 1970 which led the City of Piombino to elaborate another development plan that prohibited building on the entire promontory of Populonia and in the gulf of Baratti.

In the same period, an analogous fate did not befall the promontory of Punta Ala where the same company that proposed to lot the promontory of Populonia, obtained license to build what has become one of the largest tourist-residential complexes on the Tuscan coast.

Since then, the city's development plans have always confirmed the desire to safeguard this immense cultural and landscape heritage, supported in this by the Ministry of the Cultural and Environmental Heritage in its defense of historic-archaeological goods, and in collaboration with the Soprintendenza Archeologica per la Toscana. Since then, plans and projects have been elaborated for a park.

In 1993, the municipalities concerned by the park joined to form the "Parchi Val di Cornia," a public-private corporation with the aim of implementing and managing the Baratti-Populonia Archaeological Park, along with other parks: the San Silvestro Archaeological Mines Park in Campiglia Marittima, the Rimigliano Coastal Park in San Vincenzo, the Sterpaia Coastal Park in the commune of Piombino, the Montioni Forest Reserve in Suvereto and that of Poggio Neri in Sassetta. The Baratti and Populonia Park is the fruit of archaeological excavations conducted in the past by the Soprintendenza Archeologica and, between 1996 and 1998, by the Val di Cornia Parks Authority, under the scientific direction of Antonella Romualdi.

In her capacity as inspector for the Soprintendenza Archeologica per la Toscana, Dr. Romualdi is also credited with passionately and competently contributing to safeguarding the entire archaeological area of the promontory of Piombino.

In addition to the hard work of the Val di Cornia Parks Authority and the contributions allocated by the EEC, the park could not have been born without the positive collaboration with the Ministry of the Cultural Heritage and Activities and with the City of Piombino; a collaboration that enabled creating a single management for both state-owned and city-owned archaeological areas.

These agreements were endorsed in the convention stipulated on July 11, 1998, on the occasion of park inauguration, between the Ministry of the Cultural Heritage and Activities and the Val di Cornia Parks Authority.

This act, for the first time in Italy, licensed the use of state-owned archaeological property to a private entity, thus knocking down bureaucratic barriers that would have prevented the unitary fruition of the cultural value of this natural and archaeological site.

What we can visit today in Baratti is only the first lot of the park, and documents the necropolises and, to a small degree, the Etruscan industrial settlements.

Populonia is in reality an immense archaeological and natural park that has already offered a lot of evidence about its populations but that still holds, in its fascinating uncontaminated nature, many secrets of Etruscan, Roman and Medieval civilization.

For this reason, while it works on creating an archaeological museum of the territory of Populonia in the historic center of Piombino, the Val di Cornia Parks Authority is already examining a second phase of archaeological research and park enlargement.

All this will be possible if we are able to continue conserving the scientific and natural integrity of these places, a priceless patrimony of the national and world community.

Massimo Zucconi
President of the Val di Cornia Parks Authority

A story of sun and passion. This light, these reflections, this moving landscape. In no other place on earth does the bark of the cluster pine shine as in the golf of Baratti. On long summer's evenings, the hours of sunset in the bay of Populonia are perfect moments, suspended and unforgettable instants. The garden of pine-trees beside the beach stands out against the gently rippling waves of the Tyrrheanian Sea, while the trees swaying to the sea wind are struck by the light of the sun as it disappears at the center of the gulf. Enclosed by hills on either side where the castle of Populonia Alta and the Villa del Barone rise, the marina of Baratti is a Mediterranean enchantment. With what eyes did the Etruscans regard this sea and this extraordinary panorama? Or were they too busy smelting

The chamber tomb of the Funeral Couches in the Necropolis of San Cerbone.

The umbrella pines of the gulf of Baratti, a species that characterizes the landscape.

Elban iron to notice the world of marvel that surrounded them? To each his own personal answers to these pointless questions: not even the archaeologist has answers for these somewhat vain but inevitable interrogatives. And this land, this spared and "distant" corner of Tuscany continues to reflect mysteries and secrets. The gulf of Baratti and the hills of Populonia form a suspended landscape: one in which the beauty of the land and the memory of its history constantly disrupt the visitor. With well-deserved pride, the archaeologist views the necropolises, the superb complex of tombs scattered throughout the countryside of Populonia, while the traveler is attracted by the dreamlike semicircular gulf. A point of encounter marks this story, however, a vision shared by these two, so different viewpoints: Populonia was a thriving city, a settlement of metalworkers and merchants, a strategic port for seamen who traveled the Tyrrheanian Sea, a land of harsh toil, a challenge to life. Here, families that had grown rich and powerful decided, for their heavenly glory, to build impressive sepulchers, like the Tomb of the Chariots. The ancient vitality of Populonia relives in the passion of archaeologists, of the people who live on the promontory, of those who have fallen in love with this land and of those who desire a modern and practically unique management for a splendid Archaeological Park. A passion that has eradicated the melancholy from the journals of past travelers. Thus, discovery is simple and, at the same time surprising: the gulf of Baratti, even in the dangerous years of tumultuous change imposed by tourism, has maintained a precious balance. One you will not fail to note as you come down the hill towards the sea, away from the Via Aurelia: the surprise of the first encounter with the horizons of Baratti

is great and stunning. The gulf is a beautiful land that still arouses wonder. An observation post in the forest of Populonia looks out onto an oak-wood and the quarry of Le Grotte which, millennia ago, were transformed into an underground labyrinth of tombs. From this point, you can simultaneously grasp the image of the classical history of the Etruscan city, the coastline, the

Panoramic view of the Necropolises of Le Grotte from the observation post. In the background, the gulf of Baratti and the mountains of Campiglia.

domes formed by cluster pines and the distant profile of the mountains of Campiglia Marittima: this is the geography that determined the destiny of Populonia and

still today continues to model it. It is the perfect synthesis of this environment, the desired union between its past and present. The passion for this place is visible in the eyes of the young people who work at the Archaeological Park. A passion which, fed by a marvelous sea and exciting archaeological finds, is indeed quite contagious.

This land has never been abandoned. History of Populonia.

Capable of chipping stone and smoothing it into axes and arrowheads, man moved up to the brush of the promontory of Piombino. Paleolithic man, contemporary of the Neanderthal, began to walk the hills of Populonia and the mountains of Campiglia. The prehistoric nomad settled in the same places where, millennia later, the Etruscans built their villages. Man was never to leave this promontory.

Neolithic ceramics have been found on the crest of the hills that connect Populonia and Piombino. Eneolithic miners (III millennium BC) brought copper ore to red-hot heat in the forges of San Vincenzo. Since very remote times, this region's mining wealth began to model life, economy and survival systems. Huts with flooring made of vase fragments and walls of branches protected by clay plastering, dotted the sandy coast of the gulf of Baratti: in the shelter of sandbars, these were the settlements of the late Bronze Age (XII-X centuries BC), the villages of the area's first real population: numerous and evident traces of their settlements have been found between San Vincenzo and Baratti. The necropolis of the Villa del Barone, situated five hundred meters from the settlement of Poggio del Molino, dates to this very ancient period. In the centuries of the Bronze Age, the men of Baratti were fishermen

Distribution of finds from the Villanovan epoch in the territory of Populonia.

Hypothetical reconstruction of a settlement at the end of the Bronze Age (second half of the XII-X century BC). Generally located on the sandy coast adjoining mineral fields, these centers were formed by huts with vase fragment flooring, held together with clay, while the walls were probably made using twigs and branches and then plastered with clay.

Typologies of Villanovan Tombs

In the Villanovan epoch, the crematory rite was widespread (pozzo tombs containing biconical or ovoid urns) and already practiced since the end of the Bronze Age. The second half of the IX century saw the introduction of a burial rite with fossa tombs (with walls lined with dry masonry or stone slabs). This practice joined the crematory rite and then slowly replaced it. Towards the end of the IX century BC, the chamber tomb made its first appearance in Etruria with its corbelled dome (visible in the necropolises of Poggio delle Granate and Poggio del Mulino). We then move from the individual tomb to the one destined to the family group. This reflects the evolution of Populonian society and the affirmation of family nuclei which assumed a certain importance. Among the chamber tombs, let us mention the bronze tomb of the Crescent-shaped Razor, discovered in 1920 on the southwestern slope of Poggio delle Granate. Probably built between the end of the IX and the beginning of the VIII centuries BC, the grave was formed by a circular cell surmounted by a corbelled dome and placed at the center of a stone circle, 4 meters in diameter, at a level higher than that of the burial chamber floor.

Distribution of Necropolises

Given that till today, the remains of the ancient settlements in the area of Populonia are rather scarce, the most useful indications to understand territorial and settlement dynamics of this area are provided by the distribution of necropolises in the various historic periods.

During the Iron Age (IX-VIII centuries BC), the burial grounds in the territory of Populonia were mainly concentrated in the eastern part of the gulf of Baratti (area of Poggio and Piano delle Granate), in the center of the inlet (Casone, San Cerbone and Porcareccia where the later necropolises were also located) and on the north-western slope of Poggio del Molino or del Telegrafo, near the area of the future acropolis. This distribution has led some to hypothesize the existence of many villages, located on the heights inland of the gulf of Baratti, each with its own burial ground.

In the Orientalizing period (late VIII, early VI century BC),

the necropolises occupied portions of the pre-existing Villanovan cemeteries (Granate, Porcareccia, San Cerbone), successively extending to the hills inland of the gulf (Conchino, Campo all'Arpia, Felciaieto, Costone della Fredda, Palmente, Poggio Malassarto, Podere Casone and Poggio al Finocchio). Several of these later tombs, found in a rather limited area, might have belonged to a single necropolis, tied to the settlement on the three hills of Molino, Castello and Guardiola.

During the VI and V centuries, necropolis distribution concentrated in the central portion of the gulf of Baratti (Podere San Cerbone, Podere Casone, Porcareccia) and in the nearby areas, while the use of peripheral burial grounds (like that of Granate) used uninterruptedly since the Iron Age, ceased once and for all. This could mean the abandonment of secondary settlements and the definitive stabilization of the main settlement, in the area of the acropolis. In the Hellenistic Age, the ceaseless growth of industrial activities in the lower city made it necessary, for economic

reasons, to exploit the old burial grounds. The considerable demographic growth of this period also called for new and larger cemeteries: thus the necrop-

olises of Poggio Malassarto, Poggio delle Grotte and Buche delle Fate were created. The underground chamber tombs (hypogea) of the two latter areas were dug into the slopes of abandoned quarries or along superficial outcroppings.

Alongside these larger burial areas, use of the ancient necropolis continued (Casone, San Cerbone) as shown by the graves dug in the intermediate stratums of the iron scoria.

and gathered mollusks. They were already capable of bravely venturing into the Tyrrheanian Sea on fishing expeditions. The presence of millstones reveals an intense farming activity. Metalworking was already a column of the economy. The first merchants began to explore sea routes, even reaching Corsica and Sardinia, seeking to exchange the products of the new industry and create a promising commercial network.

In the Iron Age (IX-VII centuries BC), the inhabitants of the promontory and the surrounding plains began to stir, moving the villages and undertaking short migrations: they climbed the heights of Baratti and the promontory of Populonia. Settlements grew more numerous and scattered, while the inhabitants moved inland of the coast. Necropolises guide the research of archaeologists: the man of the Iron Age cremated his dead, the ashes were gathered in biconical vases and the grave goods were only a few objects.

The scattered villages of the Villanovan centuries slowly formed relations and exchanged experiences; contacts grew more frequent: the settlements began to grow closer to one another. The first real urban organization in the gulf of Baratti was clearly visible between the VII and VI centuries BC. In his commentary to the Aeneid (IV century AD), Servius records ancient legends affirming, in a double and contradictory hypothesis, that colonists from Corsica and Volterra founded a new city here on the seashore. In reality, only one fact is certain: Populonia was born from the unification of scattered villages. The acropolis occupied the two hills of the promontory (Poggio del Mulino and Poggio del Castello), the settlement on the western slope faced the open sea and its inhabitants

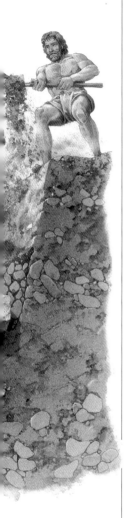

Reconstruction of a cremation burial in the Iron Age (IX-VIII centuries BC). The typical biconical Villanovan cinerary urn is covered with a bowl. In several male tombs, the covering of the vase containing the ashes was a terracotta helmet.

The City

As affirmed by ancient authors like Pliny the Elder and Strabo, Populonia was the only important Etruscan city built right on the sea. The other settlements on the coast were only port stations of larger cities (such as Caere, Vulci, Tarquinia…), located a safe distance inland. Etruscan territorial organization indeed included a series of urban agglomerates, generally located in the hills and connected by road networks quite different from the large arteries of the Romans who later colonized the provinces. Populonia was divided into two distinct nuclei, as we are informed by geographer Ptolemy of Alexandria and Strabo: the acropolis or upper city, location of the temples and public buildings (*Poplonion akron*) and the *Poplonion polis* or lower city, the area around the gulf and therefore of the port, where trade and craft activities were concentrated. The ancient acropolis included the area of the two hills, Poggio del Molino and Poggio del Castello, and the plain between them. The Soprintendenza Archeologica has conducted excavations in this area since 1980, bringing to light the remains of a sacred building of the Hellenistic Age (first half of the II century BC) north of a slightly more ancient sanctuary complex, in an area used since the VII century BC. The temple, long in shape and with a square cell and very narrow pronaos, reveals significant affinities to one of the temples on the acropolis of Volterra. The decorative apparatus too, as visible in several portions (two male heads, probably on the pediment and a fictile facing), presents shared features with terracotta figures from Volterra, as well as with those of the temple of Catona in Arezzo.

Male heads in terracotta belonging to the decoration of the Hellenistic temple on the acropolis.

The foundations of the Hellenistic temple on the acropolis of Populonia, between Poggio del Molino and Poggio del Castello (first half of the II century BC). The building has elements similar to those of one of the temples on the acropolis of Volterra.

Distribution of constructions and wells (indicated by circles) during the Hellenistic age, in the area of Populonia.

two consecutive sea raids by the Syracusans who, in 453 BC, attacked the coasts of Etruria, Elba and Corsica, probably to disturb iron routes and so weaken the power of dangerous trade rivals. The boundary wall of the acropolis surrounds the upper part of the two hills Molino and Quercioleta) has led to hypothesizing later works of maintenance and additions.

The fortification of the lower city, location of metallurgical and trade activities, was undertaken during the Hellenistic period (perhaps between the late IV and early III centuries BC). A first wall segment was unearthed in a good state of conservation in 1926 by Antonio Minto, on remaining photographs show the wall bond, made employing two types of finish, rusticated ashlar and smoother blocks. The fortification complex was formed by three arms that met on Poggio della Guardiola. From here, the first tract descended towards the gulf of Baratti, the second reached Cala S. Quirico and the third climbed up to Poggio

The Walls

The defensive system of ancient Populonia consisted in two fortification complexes, built in different epochs: the walls of the acropolis and those of the lower city. The Populonians perhaps decided to fortify the upper city following a series of episodes that occurred during the first half of the V century BC: the sea battle at Cuma in 474 BC in which the Etruscan fleet suffered a searing defeat and the

Castello, developing for a total length of about two and one-half kilometers. The structure was built using more or less square calcareous stone blocks of various sizes, arranged in irregular rows. The collapse of the upper portion prevents establishing the height of the ancient walls. The original plan of the walls should date to mid V century BC, though the technique observed in several segments (such as on the slope in the direction of Cala della

the Poggio della Guardiola, in the direction of the gulf of Baratti. The structures were erected on the rock by means of special terracing; fairly regular rows of stone from the local quarries were built with bossing on the side surfaces and a type of finish similar to the one used in the fortification of Greek centers. The new walls had turrets which were unfortunately destroyed in 1937 by the personnel charged with recovering scoria: the

Segment of the boundary wall around the acropolis of Populonia, in the locality of "I Massi," in an engraving by S.J. Ainsley (from the 1883 London edition, George Dennis, *The Cities and Cemeteries of Etruria*).

del Molino, connecting the Hellenistic walls with the more ancient walls of the acropolis.

Until today, few remains have been found of the gates in the walls in correspondence to the roads that climbed up to the city.

could admire the profile of nearby Elba Island. The city was protected by a powerful circle of walls; metalworking industrial centers rose towards mid-VI century BC on the slopes of the Poggio della Porcareccia; the coast offered safe berth to the ships that sailed the Tyrrheanian. The name of Populonia is symbol of fertility and prosperity: it comes from the Etruscan *puple*, meaning "sprout," connected with the god *Fufluns*, the Dionysus-Bacchus brought to central Italy by its new inhabitants. Indeed central Italy, between the basins of the Arno and Tiber rivers, witnessed the coming of the Etruscans, a powerful, aggressive and determined people. They were the ones to make Populonia great, the only Etruscan city on the sea, Populonia was a land with a glistening destiny: the gulf of Baratti was already a strategic crossroads, a terminal of sea traffic and commerce, a sure port on Tyrrheanian courses. Arti-

Polychrome floor mosaic found in 1842 in a vineyard over the monumental base of the Building of the Loggias. It depicts a shipwreck and probably dates to the first half of the I century BC.

sans opened shops and workshops where copper and tin from Campiglia were smelted; merchants strengthened ties with Sardinia and Corsica and traded with the most important villages of southern Etruria. The Etruscans resolutely ventured to every corner of the Mediterranean, even reaching the cities of classical Greece where they had intense contact with Samos, Rhodes, Miletos and Corinth; their ships sailed to the mouth of the Rhone, and onward to the Greek colony of Marseilles. It was the "Orientalizing" period of Etruscan culture: the superb necropolises of the gulf of

The Roman Building of the Loggias

On the north-eastern slope of Poggio del Molino or del Telegrafo, within the circle of walls that surrounded the ancient necropolis, we can see the impressive remains of a construction of the Roman epoch. An ample stone terracing, inserted into the hill slope and characterized by the presence of six large blind arches, made of an ashlar structure that leans against a wall made of sandstone blocks. The building, dated approximately I century BC on the basis of a polychrome floor mosaic portraying a scene of a shipwreck, was found in 1842 by count Giovanni Desideri and Alessandro François in a vineyard over the terracing. The construction, which has always stimulated the imagination of visitors and scholars of the past alike, has been interpreted as "Amphitheatre" (Leandro Alberti in 1550), a "beautiful and magnificent "Swimming-pool" (Giorgio Santi, physician and naturalist, in 1806), location of the city baths (Minto in 1914). Thereafter, the building has always been considered as belonging to a sea villa with a panoramic location. In reality, its central and dominant location, in addition to the arches on the base, might suggest a different type of use, perhaps sacred or public. When the excavation campaigns (Department of Archaeology, Universities of Siena and Pisa) recently undertaken around the building, have progressed, we may have further elements to identify the structure.

The arches of the monumental terracing of the Roman Building of the Loggias, on the hill of Poggio del Molino, in a photograph from the thirties.

Baratti held jewels, ceramics, precious objects made of gold, silver and vitreous paste from the eastern Mediterranean. The tombs were treasure chests containing flasks of perfumed oil, little bronze statues, weapons, helmets, tableware for banquets in the afterworld. A family of warriors buried a racing chariot and a calash with their dead. Apart from the crisis that erupted in the second half of the VIII century BC, Populonia was a vital center, the port of Etruria, a city of metallurgy, a village of industries. Her merchants controlled the copper deposits in the area of Campiglia. A class of wealthy and powerful merchants was born. They were the "princes" who controlled the commerce of metals and held the keys of power: they built impressive tombs at San Cerbone where they buried their families with splendid objects, fruit of trade in the Mediterranean. In the VI century, iron burst into the life of Populonia: a decisive thrust forward.

There was fresh water in the gulf of Baratti, woods for carbon to burn in the clay furnaces to heat Elban iron ore. Elba Island with its iron mines was just across the channel, a tract of sea no more than ten kilometers wide: a short and easy voyage for the expert sailors of the Etruscan city. The destiny of Populonia and the promontory of Piombino was marked out: here, in the lee of the sandbars of the beaches of Baratti, Elban

The Diocese

We know that Populonia was the seat of the diocese between the end of the V and the beginning of the IX centuries AD. Thus the city must have conserved its political and administrative importance in the territory, at least until 809 AD, year which marked the definitive crisis of the urban center's institutional role. The diocese was transferred, first to Cornino and then, definitively, to Massa Marittima (1062). The most famous bishop was Cerbone who later became patron saint of the city. On his escape from Elba Island in search of shelter from Lombard incursions, he requested and obtained, by divine intercession, to be buried in Populonia.

One hypothesis suggests that the first burial place of the Saint's body (later transferred to the cathedral of Massa Marittima) was the chapel of San Cerbone in Baratti. Fragments of reliefs from the High Middle Ages, reutilized in the chapel walls, traces of old wall structures and the presence of graves, witness the cultural function performed by this area since antiquity.

hematite was refined and iron was extracted from the island's minerals: in little time, the city became the most important iron center in Mediterranean antiquity, the key link of the entire economy of Etruria.

To pay for the services tied to such frenetic economic activity, it was decided (V century) to create a mint and strike coins. And the coins of Populonia with the image of the *Gorgoneion*, the mythological monster printed on the metal, spread through Etruscan lands: finds at Aleria on Elba Island, inland of the coast of Livorno, in the regions around lake Prile testify to the city's important economic influence. Money served to regulate a growing and intense mercantile exchange and to pay the soldiers who began to patrol the promontory to guarantee the safety of the Etruscan coast.

The chapel of San Cerbone in Baratti. Despite its rather recent appearance, the building reveals much more ancient origins, as shown in the relief fragments of the high Middle Ages, reused in the walls, traces of earlier wall structures and the presence of graves.

Populonia was a precious port (the exact location of the docks remains an unsolved archaeological puzzle), an indispensable port station along the courses between southern France and the south of Italy. Populonia attracted people in search of work and fortune: a relentless demographic boom began. Researchers affirm that here in a setting made red-hot by the smelting furnaces, lived more than ten thousand people, an out-and-out factory city. Where did they live? Sleep? Eat? These are questions that remain largely unsolved. Populonia has left us a memory made of tombs, but has still not totally revealed the secrets of its everyday life. We know for certain that many desperate souls came here from Spain, Sardinia, Campania and Corsica: all in search of possible survival. Populonia witnessed migrations even from Greece. The city grew: houses, new defensive walls and public buildings were built with a calcarenite stone, extracted from large quarries in the hills of the promontory and from the rocky walls of Buche delle Fate. The up-and-coming Rome in central Italy, called for iron, noble metals for its weapons and objects, and Populonia was the production center. These were the centuries of the city's greatest economic development: the IV and III centuries before Christ witnessed such fervent activity and so much iron was produced that the scoria unused by Etruscan technology covered every subsidence of the gulf of Baratti and even buried the more ancient necropolises. The economy had neither moral scruples nor past heredity to defend. New cemeteries rose at Poggio Malassarto, Le Grotte, Buche delle Fate. Unaffected by the recession that struck the other cities of Etruria, Populonia did not even feel its naval defeat by the fleet of Syracuse at Cuma in 474 BC which decreed the end of the Etruscan sea dominion in the Tyrrheanian. But Rome was conducting a pushy expansionist policy and Etruria could not withstand for long. Rome advanced northward and, through war and alliances, annexed the Etruscan territories. By the end of the III century before Christ, Populonia had come under the influence of the new power of antiquity for good. The production system was altered, the structure of Etruscan workshops overturned by an impetuous, disordered, voracious metallurgy. The II and I centuries before Christ were probably the period of the city's most impressive metallurgical activity. The iron industries of Populonia supplied the iron that armed the fleet of Publius Scipio on the eve of the expedition against Carthage (205 BC). In these same years, the Via Aurelia started climbing up towards

The "mastio" (stronghold) of the castle of Populonia. The first nucleus of this tower was probably built between the end of the XIII and beginning of the XIV centuries.

View of the castle of Populonia with its semicircular tower.

The Castle of Populonia

Sources cite a primitive castle, founded by the bishop of Massa Marittima, as of 1117 ("Porto Baronti infra ipsum castellum"). It stood at the foot of the city of Populonia near the port of Baratti, in an area which we have already seen had a certain importance also in the centuries of the High Middle Ages. The present fortified complex of the fortress and walls of Populonia was probably built at the beginning of the XV century by Gherardo Appiano who became lord of Piombino in 1399. It seems the settlement was planned to repopulate the ancient city of Populonia which, though at that time, no longer existent, was still remembered for its territorial importance as an iron center and port station.

Though the construction features of the entire system would make one think of a single opus of coordinated planning, the central tower of Populonia (the "mastio") was probably erected earlier, between the end of the XIII and the beginning of the XIV centuries. The territory of Populonia in this period was under the rule of the Pisans who, in 1305, also decided to build a new dock in the port of Baratti. This operation, aimed at

strengthening the receptivity and traffic of the ancient port, restoring it a new importance, might have included the construction of a lookout post towards the peak of the promontory, where the acropolis stood: the stronghold. The primitive nucleus of the tower was later modified adding a base "shoe" during the construc-

tion of the fortified complex in the early fourteen-hundreds, but the position of the stronghold, off-center compared to the regularity of the settlement, reveals its

greater antiquity. The present layout of Populonia is typical of settlement models in the High Middle Ages, with an orthogonal road network and the division into regular building lots with homogenous measurements. The decision to build the fifteenth-century center within the ancient circle of walls was certainly no coincidence, as shown by a part of the fortress structure, erected over a segment of the ancient stone walls, perhaps the base of a sacred building.

Since then, the fortified complex was subjected to restoration and rebuilding, though the plan remained substantially unchanged. There is news of an intervention conducted at the beginning of last century which, to restore the wall structures, employed stone blocks taken from the drum of the tomb of the Funeral Couches. Archaeological studies presently underway on the northern slope of Poggio del Castello (Department of Archaeology, Universities of Siena and Aquila), have evidenced traces of two ecclesiastical buildings, presumably attributable to the Low Middle Ages.

Pisa and touched the industrial center and harbor of the Piombino promontory. The port was a strategic seat of Roman power in the Tyrrheanian. These were also the last years of resplendence: Rome expanded and could now count on other sources for raw materials. The entire economy of central Italy began to tot-

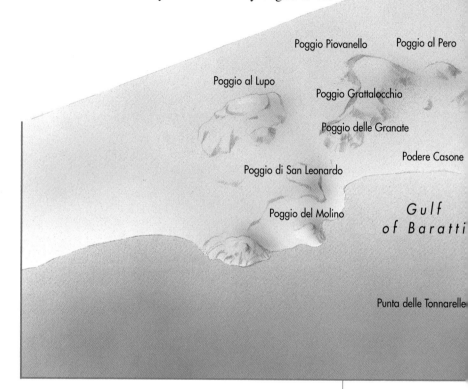

ter. Moreover, Populonia along with the other Etruscan cities chose the wrong ally in the struggle between Lucius Cornelius Sulla and Gaius Marius for power in Rome.

Around the year 80 BC, the armies of the aristocratic Sulla besieged the city, conquered it, destroyed a temple on the acropolis, executed the inhabitants and confiscated the goods of the most important families. This marked the first great crisis of the industrial epic of

oggio al Finocchio   Costone della Fredda

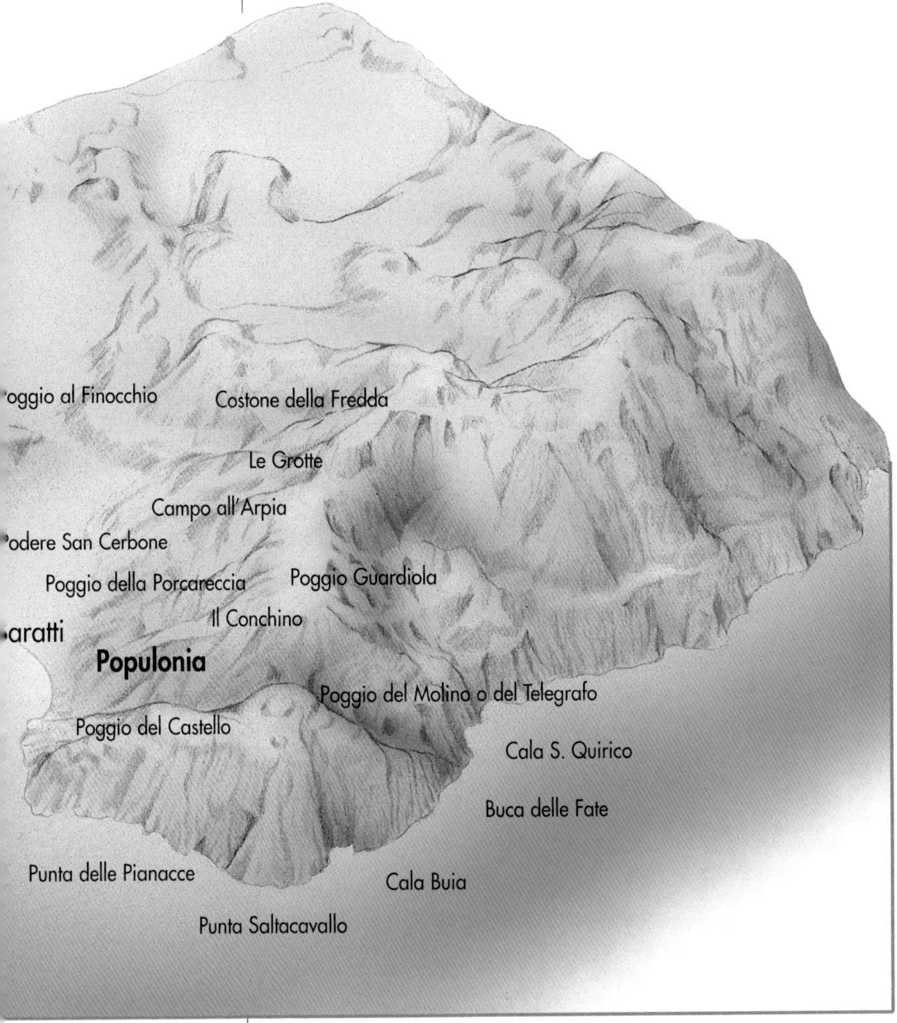

Le Grotte

Campo all'Arpia

odere San Cerbone

Poggio della Porcareccia   Poggio Guardiola

Il Conchino

aratti

Populonia

Poggio del Molino o del Telegrafo

Poggio del Castello

Cala S. Quirico

Buca delle Fate

Punta delle Pianacce

Cala Buia

Punta Saltacavallo

The territory of Populonia and the main sites of archaeological finds.

Populonia. The city never fully recovered. Only the port, thanks to the politics of Augustus, managed to survive and maintain some importance for the Tyrrheanian sea routes. But at the beginning of our era, the Greek geographer Strabo in his journals could only describe the desert of the acropolis and the city's solitude.

Only a few stubborn metalworkers continued to make Elban iron in the few remaining forges.

Lands of water and fire.

Water and fire, streams and oakwoods supplying wood and carbon: the gulf of Baratti, the hills of Populonia were fortunate lands, strategic crossroads of antiquity, mandatory stops in industrial and trading development, capable of making a city and a territory rich. Iron was the destiny of the promontory of Piombino: from centuries of prehistory to today's blast furnaces. The mountains of Campiglia, the line of hills that marks the horizon inland, concealed vast deposits of copper and lead, while across the sea, past Punta delle Pianacce and Punta di Saltacavallo, lay the cliffs of Elba Island that concealed vast deposits of hematite, a precious mineral with iron content that reached 56%. Populonia was the ideal place to exploit such extraordinary wealth: this corner of the Tuscan coast possessed the natural keys to the treasure chest of Etruscan power, the resources to exploit the main reserve of raw materials in central Italy. Copper, lead from Campiglia and iron from Elba Island were to guide this territory's economy and culture; metallurgy was to mark its history, environment and social structures. Prehistoric peoples immediately realized the rich resources of Campiglia: Eneolithic man (III millennium BC) already worked copper and traces of a mining village have been discovered very near San Vincenzo. The gatherers of mollusks and farmers at the end of the Bronze Age (XII-X centuries BC) were already expert metalworkers. In the Iron Age (IX-VIII centuries BC), man heated copper minerals red hot

A panoramic view of the gulf of Baratti visible from the road that climbs up to the town of Populonia.

and already traded these metals with Corsica and Sardinia. Elban hematite arrived in Populonia in the VI century BC. Rudimentary forges, full of iron scoria, have been found in the "industrial areas" of Poggio della Porcareccia: earlier than 530 BC, they are the first testimony of metallurgic activities tied to iron in the gulf of Baratti. All of a sudden, iron even changed the physical geography of this slope of the Piombino promontory. Fleets of ships loaded blocks of hematite along the western coast of Elba to then unload in the gulf of Baratti where, like a new artificial forest, a labyrinth of small volcanoes, grew a

Trade and Sea Traffic

a

c

b

d

Populonia was among the first Etruscan cities to have a regular coinage system in the second half of the V century BC.

The reasons must be sought in the need to coin a certain means of exchange to handle all the operations tied to the iron industry which had by then assumed considerable proportions and a complex organization. Ordinary trading activities in antiquity were indeed conducted without the use of money but instead by goods bartering. The repeated attacks by the Syracusans on the mining district in the course of the V century BC also made it necessary to resort to mercenary troops that had to be paid with the emission of public money. It is also probable that the availability of metals locally facilitated or accelerated this process.

The most ancient coins were silver: the different coin series depicted divinities such as the *Gorgoneion* (the head of the Gorgon, a monster of Greek mythology), the image of the god *Turms* (the Greek Hermes, the Roman Mercury), the hero *Hercle*, the goddess *Menrva* (the Greek Athena and Minerva of the Latins) and a male figure wearing a crown of twigs. Populonian bronze coins too, identifiable with certainty by the Etruscan name of the city (*Pupluna* or *Pufluna*), portrayed the same personages in addition to the god *Sethlans,* patron of metallurgical activities, who corresponded to the Greek Hephaestus and the Latin Vulcan, deformed husband of Venus.

The territorial distribution of finds of Populonian coins (Aleria in Corsica, Tarquinia, Vicarello, Roselle, inland of the Livorno coast, the territories of Umbria and Pistoia …) testifies to quite a vast area of economic influence.

Moreover, the only Etruscan coin found north of the Apennine Mountains, at Prestino, near Como, was a Populonian silver didrachm.

Populonia had a strategic location, at the center of the most traveled trade routes of antiquity. The connections between the eastern Mediterranean, the Greek colonies of Meridione and Massalia (today's Marseilles, founded by the Phokaians), had to pass through the city's port, as did most of the routes directed towards the upper Tyrrheanian and the sea of Liguria. Ships transported Greek and Etruscan handicrafts such as painted pottery, bucchero (the typical black ceramics), foodstuffs and, of course, iron which from the port of Populonia spread throughout the ancient world.

There is no certain news yet on the location of the port structures of Baratti because of the erosion that through the centuries has modified the profile of this segment of coast. Thanks to its natural conformation, the gulf certainly offered sure shelter from sea storms like the one that occurred in 203 BC, forcing consol Tiberius Claudius and his fleet to seek refuge in the city's port.

a) Silver didrachm with the image of Minerva (IV century BC).

b) Silver didrachm with the *Gorgoneion*.

c) Bronze sextant: front, with the image of the god *Sethlans*, patron of metallurgy.

d) Bronze sextant: back, with hammer and tongs, symbols of metallurgy.

Reconstruction of an Etruscan ship of the VII-VI century BC. Transported goods included iron (in various phases of processing), wine, oil, handcrafted products (such as Greek or Etruscan pottery) scented oils and unguents, grains.

maze of forges always lit that redrew the face of the gulf hills. Populonia became an industrial city, a city of constant activity where extraordinary fortunes were made.

The Etruscans refined an amazing metalworking technology: without thermometers, they were capable of heating the mass of iron hematite up to 1300 degrees centigrade. Too little to melt the iron completely, but enough to separate the noble part of the metal from the wastes. Without stopping a single day, the forges heated the minerals transported from Elba Island. And from Populonia, a sure port and industrial emporium of antiquity, ships departed for

Mediterranean ports: iron was the engine of a rich and relentless commerce. In little time, Populonia became the first iron center of Mediterranean antiquity. Her iron reached the villages of Sardinia and Corsica and was exchanged with precious objects and fine ceramics on the islands of Greece. Etruscan "businessmen" did business with the merchants of Samos, Corinth and Rhodes. Their ships sailed north in the Tyrrheanian up to the French coasts. Even Rome became one of the most important customers of Etruscan "businessmen": the fleet of Publius Cornelius Scipio, armed in 205 BC thanks to Populonian iron, was destined to defeat the powerful Carthage.

The years between the IV and III centuries BC marked an industrial explosion, a dazzling economic boom that burned mountains of hematite. Once again, man modified the landscape, canceling even the memory of its history. The scoria, residues of iron extraction, unusable by the technology of the time, buried the ancient necropolises, and artificial hills of blackish debris transformed the profile of the gulf of Baratti once again.

In the first centuries of Roman influence (III century BC), industrial activities became chaotic, disorganized and very intense. The unused scoria by now formed black walls along the coast. Close to three hundred thousand tons of scoria were spread over the territory between Baratti and the gulf of Follonica. But the period of Etruscan splendor was coming to an end: Imperial Rome began searching elsewhere, towards distant regions, for the raw materials she needed. It is a slow, gradual process, with ups and downs, but relentless. The crisis struck the economy of all of Italy. It was the I century AD. The crisis of Rome's iron industry is certain, though the causes and consequences on the economic and social structure remain to be further examined. During the Augustan age, Strabo the geographer still saw workers and craftsmen at work near the beach of Baratti. But decadence was evident and inevitable. In only a few decades, the iron region of antiquity became a forgotten province. The production system of

The beach of Baratti still offers visible traces of the ancient processes of iron working.

Campiglia in the High Middle Ages left unclear traces: forges situated around several castles and monasteries produced the iron necessary to forge tools for these communities. But metallurgy could not totally disappear: it is in the genetic code of these hills. Between the X and XI centuries, an authentic village of miners and foundries stood right outside Campiglia: the powerful Fortress of San Silvestro. To exploit the rich deposits of coinable metals of these hills, the Gherardesca counts created the structures of an "industrial" center, hidden by the forests inland. One of the most thrilling testimonies of the Middle Ages in Tuscany.

The deposits of Elban iron also continued to be exploited during the middle centuries of the Middle Ages: Pisa invented an original form of monopolistic control over iron production. Itinerant craftsmen, traveling blacksmiths, workers of a surprising nomadic metallurgy began to frequent the woods of upper Maremma, building precarious smelting furnaces along the courses of streams: they were the "Pisan blacksmiths," authentic freelance workers who, in specialized teams (a man at the furnace, one at the bellows, another for the fuel and a watchman) created seasonal smelting centers, heating iron minerals and producing semi-finished goods which they then sold to Pisan craftsmen to be forged. Careful research conducted in the area of Follonica has revealed the importance of the Pisan iron industry: proof of the migration of Pisan blacksmiths are found in the traces of 85 seasonal metallurgical centers, censused inland of the gulf of Follonica. Itinerant blacksmiths did not stand up to the end of the Pisan monopoly on Elban minerals and the increasing competition in improving technology: the nomadic blacksmiths disappeared at the end of the twelve-hundreds. Behind them, they left some 26,000 tons of iron scoria. In just short of two centuries, they had smelted 16,000 tons of iron.

In the course of the XIV century, hydraulic energy produced by mills overwhelmed the old iron industry: public authorities immediately intuited the importance of these new iron production capabilities

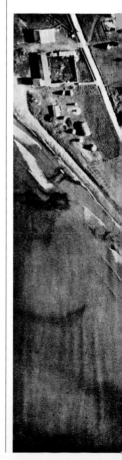

Aerial view of the necropolises of San Cerbone and Porcareccia around 1940, during the recovery of iron scoria. You can see the shapes of the tombs emerging from the scoria, industrial warehouses below, and the building which today hosts the Park Documents Center.

and metallurgical centers sprang up throughout the territory. The furnaces of Populonia were not relit and metallurgy found its capitals between Follonica and the area around Campiglia. The power of the Medicis on Elba Island was to form an unassailable monopoly on the mineral resources of Tuscany: Cosimo dei Medici launched a process to concentrate iron production plants. The first steps towards the blast furnaces of today's Piombino. The iron industry changed the promontory slope: from north to south, from the gulf of Baratti to the gulf of Follonica. Like an unseemly inheritance, the black hills of

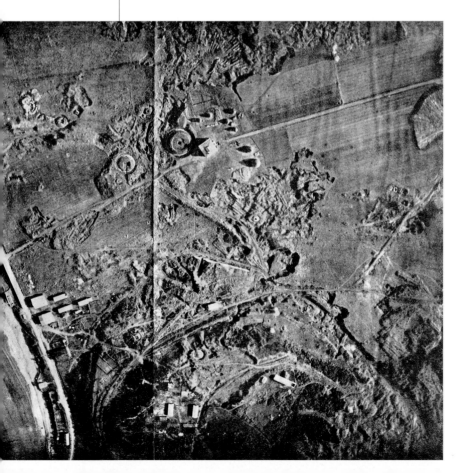

The Etruscans and Ironworking

"Near the city called Populonia lies an island of Etruria called Aithalia ("the smoky": Elba) which, lying only 100 stadia away, took its name from the great quantity of soot found there. It indeed possesses iron mineral in great quantities and of fine quality that is broken into pieces for smelting to obtain iron. Workmen break the stones and burn the many pieces in furnaces perfectly de-

vised: smelting them here with great fires, dividing the stones by size and making pieces similar to large sponges... Some purchase the ware and assemble a multitude of blacksmiths who work it into many objects of iron, fashioning weapons and hoes, sickles and other tools. And as merchants spread these things in every place, many are the lands of the world

that profit thereby." This passage by Diodorus Siculus, Greek author of the I century BC, describes the ironworking conducted in antiquity on Elba Island. In reality, from the remains of the industrial district of Porcareccia, the mineral is known to have been also processed in Populonia at least since the VI century.

Techniques of Transforming Iron Mineral

Iron is a chemical element that abounds in nature. It makes up about 5% of the materials of the earth's crust. Iron ores are many and of many types. The main ones include the oxides (magnetite, hematite), the hydroxides (limonite) and the carbonates (siderite). The Elban mineral used in the furnaces of Populonia was hematite.

Roasting and Grinding

The mineral can generally not be used as it is found in nature. An initial treatment often seeks to increase its quality by eliminating the sterile parts it contains. These preliminary treatments are both mechanical (selection, washing, grind-

ing) and thermal (roasting).

Reducing the Mineral

In mines, iron is found combined with other elements. The operation that enables separating the iron from the other components is called "reduction." In antiquity, reduction was conducted following the so-called "direct" method by means of which the gangue, at 1100-1300°C, reaches the melting point and forms a liquid

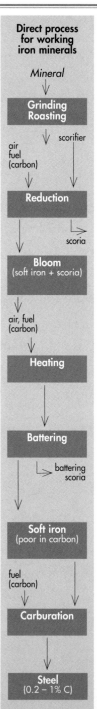

(scoria), while the metallic iron remains solid but soft (melting point of iron: 1536°C). In this moment, the liquid can be separated rather easily. The

---

Direct process for working iron minerals

Mineral
↓
Grinding Roasting
↓   ↘ scorifier
air fuel (carbon) ↓   ↓
Reduction
↓   ↘ scoria
Bloom (soft iron + scoria)
↓
air, fuel (carbon) ↓
Heating
↓
Battering
↓   ↘ battering scoria
Soft iron (poor in carbon)
↓
fuel (carbon) ↓
Carburation
↓
Steel (0.2 – 1% C)

direct method was systematically used until the XIV century. The final product of the reduction process using the direct method is a block of impure metal mixed with scoria and carbon which is defined as tuff (or bloom). Before subjecting tuff to forging, it must be further purified. This refining is performed by heating the tuff and compacting it little by little by hammering. The scoria still present is smelted again and accumulates on the furnace floor. The final product is a mass of forgeable iron.

Forging Iron

The true purpose of forging is to give shape to an object and, at the same time, give the metal the desired physical characteristics (hardness, flexibility, resistance to compression, torsion, friction, corrosion, etc.) depending on its intended use. Practically all of these aspects can be determined during forging.

Hypothetical reconstruction of the furnaces used by the ancients to smelt iron. The walls were made of firestone stuccoed with clay. The oxygen needed was introduced by means of bellows inserted in special holes and the mineral was arranged in alternating layers with wood carbon.

scoria that the Etruscans were not able to smelt, remained in Populonia.

The black hills

One century ago, the gulf of scoria was a surreal setting. In the early 1900s, the extraordinary beauty of the sea of Baratti fought a bitter battle of colors: the Tyrrheanian blue versus black mountains of iron that

had accumulated only a few meters from the beach. The inheritance of the Etruscan and Roman iron industry was stunning: they had abandoned an ocean of debris on the hills of Populonia. Two and one-half million tons of scoria covered more than two hundred thousand square meters: black hills of 1,125,000 cubic meters of debris, exceptional symbol of the appalling undertakings of the ancients.

A steam shovel at work on Poggio della Porcareccia during scoria recovery.

The mining engineers of this century could not believe their eyes: incapable of extracting every gram of useful iron from hematite, the Etruscans with the wastes of their metallurgical fires had formed an immense open-air mine. The scoria that had changed the geography of the gulf of Baratti, even covering the

View of the gulf and installations for exploiting the scoria.

large tombs of the Etruscan necropolises, still contained 60% of noble metal. Too much to abandon, too much not to exploit one more time. Belgium and Britain laid eyes on those deposits of iron. Italy too, between the two World Wars, needed it. The recovery of the Etruscan waste began in 1921. Steam shovels demolished the mountains of debris, little narrow-gauge railways and conveyor belts transferred the scoria to the sea where silos capable of containing up to two hundred thousand tons were built. The women of Piombino with their wide black skirts manually selected the mineral. Every fragment of metal was recovered. The iron followed the same course, this time inverted, it had followed on the Etruscan ships: it re-

Artificial landfill behind the tower of Baratti.

turned to Elba Island, filled the mineral warehouses of Rio Marina and were then loaded into the hulls of new merchant vessels. From beneath a blanket of scoria, at times ten meters high, appeared the lost tombs of the Etruscan necropolises. Iron returned buried treasures. In twelve years, between 1921 and 1932, almost three hundred thousand tons of iron scoria were removed from the beach of Baratti.

The people of Piombino worked on recovering the scoria until 1958. It took almost forty years to exhaust the scoria produced in more than a millennium by the peoples who inhabited this promontory in antiquity. In 1969, the Ferromin mining company officially forfeited the state concession to exploit Etruscan scoria. The iron epoch of Populonia which had begun three millennia before Christ was now truly over.

Disappointed Travelers.

Harsh and bitter descriptions. In their chronicles, ancient travelers only noted the solitude and the desert of Populonia. "It is not possible to make out the remains of past epochs; ravenous time has destroyed the great walls": Claudius Rutilius Namazianus, imperial poet and messenger, arrived in Populonia in 417 and was assailed by melancholy. There was no trace of the ancient industrial emporium: the city had vanished, disappeared almost into nothingness. For Namazianus, it is the proof that "cities can die." Already four centuries before Namazianus, Strabo the geographer and envoy of Augustus had been stunned by the solitude of Populonia: he wrote that only remains of walls and a few humble dwellings remained. He also noted that near the port, only few metalworkers obstinately continued to feed forges. The city already refused to rouse. Though it did launch admonishments to whomever could see them: Zaccaria Zacchi, sculptor from Volterra, confided to Dominican friar Leandro Alberti in the mid 1500s that amidst "thick woods and bush and thorns," there in the forest of the gulf of Baratti, one could find "pieces of noble marbles, capitals, bases, slabs of stone." In 1806, physician and naturalist Giorgio Santi explored the Populonia inland and shook his head: "The remains of the city are not many. Nor significant. Vain are all searches in this place." In the mid 1800s, British diplomat George Dennis followed cattle trails, forded swamps, eluded packs of wild dogs, detoured to the beach and walked on uncontaminated sand and all this, to reach the castle of Populonia. Dennis too, was struck by the remoteness of this corner of Tuscany: "Not a sail, nor a boat passed over the waters which only reflected a crown of yellow dunes." And the promontory that closed the gulf of Baratti could only be "gloomy." The diplomat briefly adds: "Few are the ancient remains of Populonia." Pioneer archaeologists had no better fortune: the first excavations by Alessandro François (1840) and Noel des Vergers (1850) were disappointing. Even the famous Schliemann, attracted by the lost fame of Populonia, searched for buried remains but to no avail. The industrial capital of Etruscan lands eluded discovery.

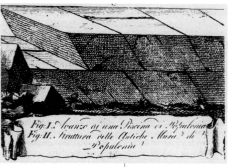

Fig: I. Avanzo di una Piscina di Populonia
Fig: II. struttura delle Antiche Mura di Populonia

TOMBS BENEATH THE SCORIA
The Season of Discoveries

And yet, fragments of the glory of Populonia began to crop up: evidence of the city's grandeur emerged in exciting casual finds. In 1832, a bronze statue, more than one meter high, was caught in the nets of Piombino fishermen off Punta delle Tonnarelle: a perfect and beautiful work. It was baptized the *Apollo of Piombino* and is today in the Louvre. In 1889, count Curzio Desideri, owner of an estate in Populonia, ordered the building of a new farmhouse facing the sea of Baratti which today hosts the Archaeological

The arches of the Roman Building of the Loggias on Poggio del Molino, and a detail of the walls around the acropolis, depicted in two engravings of the early eighteen-hundreds in *Viaggio Terzo per le due Province Senesi* by Giorgio Santi, published in 1806 in Pisa.

Park Visitors Center. It was this decision that unintentionally marked the archaeological destiny of Populonia.

During the earthwork conducted to build a road that led to this farm, physician and impassioned archaeologist Isidoro Falchi, who was to go down in history as the discoverer of Vetulonia, noted a square stone: the sandstone slab that concealed a cyst tomb. This was the first real trace of Populonia. Falchi, however, overly absorbed in his searches around Vetulonia and in bitter dispute with count Desideri, was incautious and underestimated the discovery. Such was not the case with the farmers of Baratti who dug frenetically, opened tombs and rummaged around the first discovery, finding bronze statues and gold jewels, Orientalizing ceramics and blackened lamps. Rapacious antique dealers began to commute to the gulf of Baratti to buy these sensational finds from the poor farmers. Falchi did not fail to note the objects offered in the hole-and-corner markets of Maremma and with some delay, finally realized his mistake. He returned to Populonia at the head of a team of seven workmen, headed by a foreman named Libeccio, and on November 24, 1897 began to dig the lands of the farm at San Cerbone. Ten days excavating unearthed five tombs, a sarcophagus and the walls of the large tomb of the "funeral couches": this was the lost necropolis of Populonia. The archaeological adventure of the most important industrial city of the Etruscan world had truly begun: So began the incursion of archaeologists, grave robbers, antique dealers and workmen engaged in recovering scoria to see who would be the first to uncover extraordinary treasures.

For years, museum superintendents and directors purchased objects stolen from tombs from antique dealers. In 1903, in the same point where Falchi had dug, grave-robbing farmers were the first to admire the exceptional scenes of seduction and erotism painted on the sides of two hydrias, splendid vases used to contain water for wellborn women of Populonia. It was an extraordinary and sensational find: director of the Archaeological Museum of Florence, Luigi Milani conducted difficult negotiations to purchase the two vases from Mannelli, an antique dealer in Campiglia.

Finally, in 1908, the first official excavation campaign began: three months of searching around San Cerbone unearthed the famous statue *the Suicide of Ajax*. Then came the determined years of Antonio Minto, famous superintendent to the Antichità d'Etruria, who began excavating in Populonia in 1914. He practically immediately unearthed the powerful structure of the monumental tomb of the Chariots, and other discoveries followed. A race against time: mining companies had decided to recover Etruscan iron and intended to gut the mountains of debris that the ancients had accumulated on the hills of Populonia. Steam shovels began digging in the twenties: the layer of scoria concealed the most ancient necropolis of Populonia where the tombs were like round oases in a sea of iron debris. But while steam shovels unearthed incredible monuments, they also destroyed precious testimonies of the Etruscan world. For years, every spring witnessed excavations stubbornly resume at San Cerbone, Poggio della Porcareccia, Poggio del

Conchino and Poggio della Guardiola. A struggle was engaged with grave robbers and the machines of the mining companies. The Tomb of the Cylindrical Pyxides appeared in 1928, the Tomb of the Bronze

1957 photograph of the excavations at the Tomb of the Bronze Figurine of an Offering-bearer.

Fans (Tomba dei Flabelli di Bronzo), in 1928. All activity came to a halt with World War II. Excavations and iron scoria recovery resumed, almost simultaneously, in the fifties. The photos show the mountains of Etruscan waste accumulated along the coast of Baratti: a lunar image in one of the most beautiful points of the Tyrrheanian coast. In famous photographs, workmen pose with their shov-

els on the roof of the aediculum tomb on the Podere
Casone, almost on the seashore: a corner of the sepulcher appears from under seven meters of scoria. An
exceptional document: the Bronze Figurine of an
Offering-bearer was found in front of this tomb.
Though sacked in antiquity, the tomb's structure
remained intact. It was 1957. That same year, the
first scuba-diver archaeologists found the remains of
a shipwreck of almost two thousand years ago, on
the seafloor of Baratti.

Excavations explored every corner of the gulf: the
slopes of Poggio di Porcareccia, the crags already violated by grave robbers of the necropolises of Le
Grotte and on Poggio Malassarto, all without success.
In 1967, in the woods surrounding the ancient stone
quarries where the Etruscans took the stone to build
the city's walls and palaces as well as the tombs of the
necropolises, two frescoed chamber tombs (hypogea)
were explored: the only painted tombs of Populonia.
A fisherman from San Vincenzo in 1968 found the
stunning Amphora of Baratti, a splendid vase dating to
the late IV century AD. Between 1955 and 1980, several "industrial buildings" of working class Populonia
were brought to light: on the hill of Porcareccia, they
testify to the life of the city's working class population. The last excavations campaigns, conducted between 1996 and 1998, unearthed the resplendent beauty of the labyrinth of tombs of Le Grotte.

How wrong early visitors had been, not intuiting the
mysteries of this city, resuming their travels accompanied by melancholic memories: Populonia instead
possessed thousands of secrets to reveal. And it has
barely begun to recount its past.

Detail from the *Tabula Peutingeriana* (Medieval copy from a late Roman original). Like a road map, it records distances between locations, advised stops and points of reference, such as Populonia.

Populonia Recounted by the Ancients

In his comment to Virgil's Aeneid, referring to the foundation of Populonia, the IV century AD Latin author Servius informs that, as widely held in antiquity, Populonia was the last of the twelve Etruscan cities founded by a population from Corsica or by the inhabitants of Volterra who conquered it from the Corsicans. Archaeological reality, however, disclaims these affirmations, showing that the territory of Populonia was inhabited uninterruptedly since much earlier epochs. The legend of the city's foundation probably originated from the close trade ties it had with Volterra and Corsica. Many authors (such as Diodorus Siculus, pseudo-Aristotle, Varro, Strabo) dealt with the activity for which Populonia was famous in the ancient world: ironworking. For several of them, the transformation of iron was initially performed directly at the hematite mines on Elba Island which became known as Aithalia (the smoky) for the smoke that rose from the forges where the mineral was smelted. Successively, for logical reasons (such as the presence of an important port or the availability of wood), ironworking activities were transferred to Populonia from whence the material was then distributed throughout the ancient world.

In the Aeneid, Virgil includes the city among the Etruscan allies of Aeneas: the news is of course without historic foundation but suggests the consideration the city still enjoyed in the I century BC. In his *Naturalis Historia*, Pliny the Elder (I century AD) described a very ancient statue of Jupiter, found in Populonia, made from a single, very large vine stock. Between 415 and 417 AD, poet and imperial functionary Rutilius Namazianus, visiting Populonia on his way back to Gaul, wrote of a by then completely abandoned city, the decadence of which led him to make a bitter consideration on the transience of all things. In reality, we know that while the acropolis in this period had indeed been abandoned, activities continued in the lower city and in the port, though less compared to the past. The name of Populonia is also cited in the *Tabula Peutingeriana*, the Medieval copy of a sort of "road map" of the late Roman epoch. It contains the distances between locations in miles, as well as inns and rest stations for travelers on the imperial road system.

The Park Visit

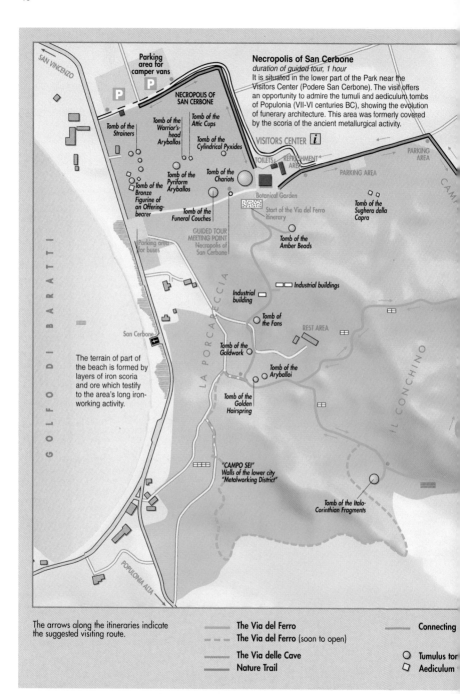

Necropolis of San Cerbone
duration of guided tour, 1 hour
It is situated in the lower part of the Park near the Visitors Center (Podere San Cerbone). The visit offers an opportunity to admire the tumuli and aediculum tombs of Populonia (VII-VI centuries BC), showing the evolution of funerary architecture. This area was formerly covered by the scoria of the ancient metallurgical activity.

SAN VINCENZO

Parking area for camper vans

P P

NECROPOLIS OF SAN CERBONE

Tomb of the Strainers

Tomb of the Warrior's-head Aryballos

Tomb of the Attic Cups

Tomb of the Cylindrical Pyxides

VISITORS CENTER [i]

TOILETS REFRESHMENT AREA

PARKING AREA

PARKING AREA

Tomb of the Pyriform Aryballos

Tomb of the Chariots

Tomb of the Bronze Figurine of an Offering-bearer

Botanical Garden

Tomb of the Sughera della Capra

Tomb of the Funeral Couches

Start of the Via del Ferro itinerary

CAMP...

GUIDED TOUR MEETING POINT
Necropolis of San Cerbone

Tomb of the Amber Beads

Parking area for buses

LA PORCARECCIA

Industrial buildings

Industrial building

San Cerbone

Tomb of the Fans

REST AREA

The terrain of part of the beach is formed by layers of iron scoria and ore which testify to the area's long iron-working activity.

Tomb of the Goldwork

Tomb of the Aryballoi

IL CONCHINO

Tomb of the Golden Hairspring

"CAMPO SEI"
Walls of the lower city
"Metalworking District"

Tomb of the Italo-Corinthian Fragments

GOLFO DI BARATTI

POPULONIA ALTA

The arrows along the itineraries indicate the suggested visiting route.

——— The Via del Ferro

- - - The Via del Ferro (soon to open)

——— The Via delle Cave

——— Nature Trail

——— Connecting

○ Tumulus tor

⬠ Aediculum

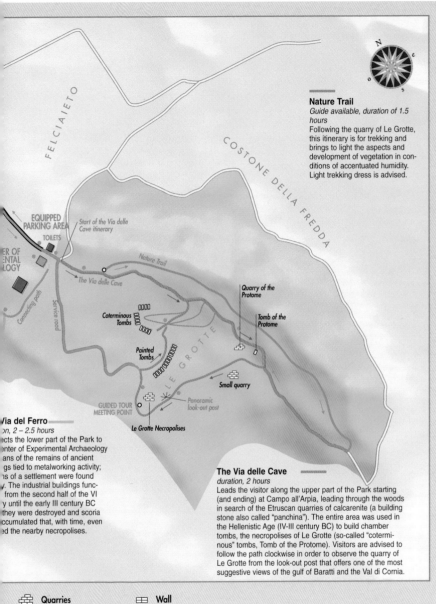

Nature Trail
Guide available, duration of 1.5 hours
Following the quarry of Le Grotte, this itinerary is for trekking and brings to light the aspects and development of vegetation in conditions of accentuated humidity. Light trekking dress is advised.

FELCIAIETO

COSTONE DELLA FREDDA

EQUIPPED PARKING AREA

TOILETS

Start of the Via delle Cave itinerary

ER OF
ENTAL
LOGY

Connecting path

service road

Nature Trail

The Via delle Cave

Quarry of the Protome

Coterminous Tombs

Tomb of the Protome

Painted Tombs

LE GROTTE

Small quarry

GUIDED TOUR MEETING POINT

Panoramic look-out post

Le Grotte Necropolises

Via del Ferro
on, 2 – 2.5 hours
ects the lower part of the Park to
enter of Experimental Archaeology
ans of the remains of ancient
gs tied to metalworking activity;
ns of a settlement were found
y. The industrial buildings func-
from the second half of the VI
y until the early III century BC
they were destroyed and scoria
ccumulated that, with time, even
ed the nearby necropolises.

The Via delle Cave
duration, 2 hours
Leads the visitor along the upper part of the Park starting (and ending) at Campo all'Arpia, leading through the woods in search of the Etruscan quarries of calcarenite (a building stone also called "panchina"). The entire area was used in the Hellenistic Age (IV-III century BC) to build chamber tombs, the necropolises of Le Grotte (so-called "coterminous" tombs, Tomb of the Protome). Visitors are advised to follow the path clockwise in order to observe the quarry of Le Grotte from the look-out post that offers one of the most suggestive views of the gulf of Baratti and the Val di Cornia.

⬛ Quarries   ⊞ Wall

◫◫◫ Tombs

● ● Waste bins

THE PARK VISITORS CENTER

The Visitors Center building develops over two floors: the ticket desk, bathroom facilities, bookshop, information office and an electronic totem pole enabling a virtual visit to all of the Val di Cornia parks, are located on the ground floor. Here too, a series of panels reconstructs the environment and history of Etruscan and Roman Populonia. The second floor of this old farmhouse hosts the areas devoted to learning activities and a video room. Found intact in 1998 in the necropolis at Le Grotte, Tomb 14 has been reconstructed here, awaiting transfer to the new archaeological museum of Cittadella in Piombino.

WORKSHOP OF EXPERIMENTAL ARCHAEOLOGY

An archaeological park must make a bet on life, revive and convey the past and show the stages of an extraordinary material culture created by man. A park must reconstruct the environments and techniques that enabled the development of a people and ancient societies. How did prehistoric man manage to make holes in the walls of steatite, a soft soaprock? How did proto-historic peoples model clay into beautiful ceramics? How did Neolithic hunters manage to chip flintstone to make their deadly arrowheads and refined ornaments such as pendants, rings or bracelets? For years, here in Populonia, experts have passionately studied the techniques that enabled prehistoric and proto-historic man to build objects, utensils, tools and jewels. Today, in the Experimental Archaeology workshop of the Baratti and Populonia Park, they revive the workshops of the peoples who

for years inhabited the promontory of Piombino. Seven millennia before Christ, the Neolithic craftsmen of Baratti chipped flintstone and jasper, drilled steatite with a surprising "bow drill," polished "jewels" using animal hides softened with saliva. The proto-historic maker of ceramics, craftsman of the Bronze Age centuries, did not know the lathe (which was instead well known to the Etruscans), but he modeled clay with his thumbs in concentric circles, using a technique which years later would come to be known as "colombine" from the name of the craftsmen, Colombini,

The Park Visitors Center

A group of children at work in the Experimental Archaeology Workshop

who in modern times again used it to make vases and amphorae. There is also a reconstruction of a kiln at the Experimental Archaeology workshop of Populonia Park that enables both students and Park visitors to fire the ceramics they have made.

The San Cerbone Farm

At the end of the eighteen-hundreds, count Curzio Desideri was the lord of Populonia: for more than a century, his family had owned a boundless estate, a vast territory that stretched from the sea to the Piombino plain. The lands between the castle of Populonia and the rivers of the Val di Cornia were his. The Bishop's Revenue of Massa and Populonia had transferred the reserve of Baratti to the Desideri counts in 1798. In 1889, on a hill near the beach of Baratti, Curzio Desideri built a large farmhouse which was to be known as the farmhouse of San Cerbone. The photographs of the period show a solid, square building, typical of the rural architecture of Maremma, with a large arched entrance and a grapevine that climbs up one side. The farm is surrounded by cultivated fields. Farmers in white

shirts pose with cattle in front of the house. A running track from the stall facilitates removing manure on a trolley. The discovery of Etruscan Populonia revolves around the construction of San Cerbone. A road had to be built to connect the farmhouse to the main road that ran inland of the beach. In the course of the earthwork to build this secondary road, a square stone was unearthed. Physician-archaeologist Isidoro Falchi did not let this find slip by him and rapidly organized excavations around the new farm: thus in 1889 appeared a first cyst tomb with its funeral goods still intact. The house at San Cerbone had indeed been built in the middle of the most important archaeological area of Populonia.

One of the most important buildings of the farm, with the end of Desideri ownership, the house became the living quarters of the "Populonia Società Italica," new owners of the area until the Archaeological Park opened. With its history and rustic beauty, the farmhouse at San Cerbone could not but become the Visitors Center of the Baratti and Populonia Archaeological Park. No longer inhabited by sharecroppers or guardians, it is instead the entrance to this lovely park in Upper Maremma. The old road that led from the coastal road to the farmhouse is still there: it grazes the large tombs of the Etruscan necropolis and enables visits to the one that conserves the name of San Cerbone.

An old picture (1914) of the farmhouse that today hosts the Visitors Center. Excavations underway on the Tomb of the Chariot can be seen on the lower right.

Ceramics were decorated using simple tools: a bone or the valve of a seashell to impress refined geometries on the still fresh clay.

Images of deer, small palm trees, ringlets and rhombuses were impressed on the curvature of vases by means of stamps fashioned from bone, bronze or ivory and today reconstructed by park researchers.

The time spent in the Experimental Archaeology workshop can truly familiarize us with the daily life of the villages that populated Baratti thousands of years before Christ.

The Necropolises of San Cerbone and Casone

This is the monumental necropolis of Populonia where the most famous tombs of the gulf of Baratti are found. Here, on the road that was to lead to the San Cerbone farm, in 1889 Isidoro Falchi noted the sandstone slab that concealed a tomb. Here, this impassioned physician-archaeologist brought to light the first structures of the tomb of the Funeral Couches and, eight years later with the help of ten workmen, began excavating to unveil the mysteries of the only city the Etruscans had built on the sea. In the Hellenistic Age (IV-III centuries BC), the necropolis had been submerged by heaps of iron scoria, produced by the frenetic smelting activity conducted in every corner of Populonia. Extraordinary aerial photographs of the fields just inland of the gulf of Baratti in the forties show the large circles of the tombs of San Cerbone which reappear, as in a mirage, in the desert of iron scoria heaped by steam shovels. Guided visits conducted over the circuit of necropolises of San Cerbone and Casone, start out from the meeting point next to the Tomb of the Chariots. Visit duration: one hour.

The area of the Necropolis of San Cerbone; in the foreground, the Tomb of the Chariots and, in the distance, the gulf of Baratti.

Right beside the Visitors Center, the old farmhouse of San Cerbone, the false dome of the **Tomb of the Chariots** looks somewhat like an Etruscan spaceship right out of the VII century BC. To bend over and pass through the hall of this tomb is one of the great emotions of Populonia. The largest and most spectacular, the Tomb of the Chariots measures close to thirty meters in diameter. Here, a powerful family had buried its dead along with the symbols of their glory: a racing chariot and a calash were walled inside the cells that line the corridor

leading to the burial chamber. Wonderful decorations in iron (a noble metal in those years) were inset in the bronze lamina that covered the sides of the chariot. Proof that Populonia was not only the site of an intense industrial activity but also one of expert craftsmen capable of modeling genuine masterpieces in metal. It was excavated between 1914 and 1921. The vault had collapsed and the tomb had already been looted, perhaps by the workmen employed at the Etruscan forges in the IV-III centuries BC.

The little plain of San Cerbone, in springtime covered with flowers and the scent of Mediterranean underbrush, rolls gently towards the sea. The tombs are scattered over this field, by now emblematic of the Etruscan universe. The marina of the gulf of Baratti is a perfect and dazzling backdrop. Here you can truly relive, and almost see, the processions that accompanied the potentates of Populonia to their sumptuous tombs: from the heights of the acropolis, the citizens in silence could view these long and solemn ceremonies. On the other hand, it is difficult to imagine that two, three centuries later, other Etruscans buried the monuments of their ancestors under iron scoria, transforming the ancient necropolis into an industrial waste area. The scoria was often so heavy that it broke through the grave domes but, at the same time, the residues of this ceaseless smelting activity also formed a protective shell for the tombs of the necropolis of San Cerbone.

The **Tomb of the Funeral Couches** was the compass that guided the first pioneering adventures of archaeologists at Populonia. Its powerful structures were discovered by the workmen of Isidoro Falchi

Bronze statue portraying Ajax in the moment of his suicide. It is dated to 500-480 BC and was found in the vicinity of the Tomb of the Funeral Couches.

Tumulus Tombs with Drum

The Tomb of the Chariots

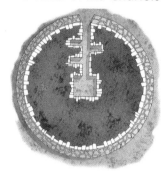

Plan of the Tomb of the Chariots. Along the corridor, small cells where grave goods were placed.

The appearance of this tomb typology during the Orientalizing epoch (VII century BC), documents the social changes that occurred in the territory of Populonia: this period indeed witnessed the formation of groups devoted to different activities, tied to trade and ironworking, which occupied separate sectors of the gulf of Baratti.

This type of tomb consists of a circular drum, generally made of blocks of "panchina" (a type of calcarenite extracted from the nearby quarries of Le Grotte), squared into blocks and dry-walled, surmounted by a corbelled dome formed by slabs of "alberese" (a type of locally found limestone), arranged in concentric circles that progressively narrowed until the elimination of rain water, employing a system practically identical to that of modern dripstones. All and any infiltration could indeed prove dangerous because of the lack of foundations, considering that the drum rested directly on natural clay. Despite the breadth of the external tumulus, which in the Tomb of the Chariots reaches 28 meters, the effective dimensions of the

closing the room. The corbelled dome was then covered with compressed soil to protect and insulate the structure, thus delineating the characteristic tumulus shape, surrounded by a containing ring made of panchina blocks. Ancient builders employed several devices to avoid damage deriving from rain water. Around the base, for example, a sidewalk of alberese stone slabs inclined away from the structure to enable water to drain off. At the juncture between the drum and the tumulus too, a system of alberese stone slabs, the *grundarium* and the *subgrundarium*, enabled

stone that are still visible today in many of the tombs. The join between the square cell and the corbelled dome above was ensured by special structures made of inclined and jutting alberese stone slabs, called "pendentives." The burial chamber is entered through the *dromos*, a corridor, often oriented eastward and covered with slabs of alberese stone which, after each burial, was sealed by means of

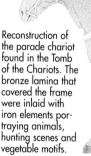

Reconstruction of the parade chariot found in the Tomb of the Chariots. The bronze lamina that covered the frame were inlaid with iron elements portraying animals, hunting scenes and vegetable motifs.

chamber that housed the dead were quite small. The room was square or rectangular and often contained funeral couches on which the dead were laid. The couches were made using slabs of panchina stone embedded into the floor to resemble the ancient beds called *klinai*: the wooden feet of the royal models were reproduced by small columns in panchina

stones and earth to protect it from being violated. Along the inner walls of the dromos, there were generally small rectangular or square cells which, destined to laying out the tomb goods, were sealed with alberese stone slabs. In addition to the Tomb of the Chariot and that of the Funeral Couches, other examples of this tomb typology are the Tomb of the Italo-

drical Pyxides) in which the entrance juts out from the drum to form an external volume that gives the entrance a more important aspect. The Tomb of the Goldwork also reveals a peculiarity: the drum is not formed by blocks of panchina stone but instead by small alberese slabs. Following an assessment performed by the Department of Tectonics of the University of Florence between 1989 and 1993, the Tomb of the Chariots was subjected to interventions of static-structural recovery in order to improve the system of damp-proofing and rain-water drainage on the tumulus surface. In July 1999, work was resumed to complete

Corinthian Fragments, at Conchino, and those of the Pyriform Aryballos, Warrior's-head Aryballos and Amber Beads. Also belonging to this typology is the Tomb of the Bronze Fans whose entrance is flanked by two limestone stele, apparently without inscriptions or decorations. A variation of the tumulus tomb is the one with a "forebody" (Tomb of the Cylin-

draining operations and improve the internal lighting system. To make the reconstructed portions recognizable, the vault in synthetic resin made in the course of restoration operations, will be painted blue, a practice by now widespread in all interventions of this type.

The Tomb of the Chariots with its 28-meter diameter is the largest of the necropolis.

Metal chariot wheels from the Tomb of the Chariots, VII century BC.

Chamber tomb of the "Funeral Couches." Slabs of panchina stone were used as bases of the beds on which the dead were lain.

during the first excavations of the necropolis. It was the year 1897, but the physician-archaeologist did not succeed in following up his studies, nor did he intuit the importance of the discovery: a conflict with count Curzio Desideri, owner of the lands, blocked Falchi's ambitions. It was only in 1908, during the first real campaign of official excavations conducted by the Superintendency to Museums and Excavations of Etruria, that it was possible to explore this large sepulcher and clean off the "feet" of the stone beds where lay the bodies of the dead, wrapped in white cloth.

Built in the VII century BC, the tomb had already been sacked in antiquity. Archaeologists only found a precious earring in gold filigree. They did, however, make an extraordinary and fortunate find amidst the mass of scoria that covered

The Tomb of the Cylindrical Pyxides in the Necropolis of San Cerbone.

Sarcophagus tombs in the Necropolis of Podere Casone. This type of grave was used in Populonia as of the VI century BC.

the roof of the tomb: a little bronze figure portraying the Greek hero Ajax in the moment of his suicide.

The **Tomb of the Cylindrical Pyxides** (a pyxis is a small case) is small and snug. Its flooring is original, though such is not the case with part of its walls which were replaced by archeologists in the twenties using travertine stone. The two pyxides

Interior of the "Tomb of the Cylindrical Pyxides" in the Necropolis of San Cerbone.

probably held objects of female cosmetics and came from Corinth.

Four wine cups, made by Greek ceramists, have given a name to the **Tomb of the Attic Cups** (VI-IV centuries BC). When it was discovered in 1925, practically nothing remained of this aediculum tomb. It had already been violated, sacked and buried by scoria. Only the traces of its base were still evident. The **Tomb of the Pyriform Aryballos** (*aryballos* is the Greek word for unguent container)

Aediculum Tombs

Tomb of the Bronze Figurine of an Offering-bearer

The aediculum tomb typology was introduced in Populonia around 560-550 BC, perhaps in relation to social changes underway in the city, when an organized structure to exploit iron resources began to take shape.

In this case, aediculum tombs, inspired by a scale representation of contemporary sacred and public buildings, were destined to a ruling class within the community. The only example of this typology found integral is the Tomb of the Bronze Figurine of an Offering-bearer which, unearthed in 1957, had already been violated perhaps by the iron workmen who in the III century BC occupied this area. The funeral monument occupies a particularly important location at a crossroads of two cemetery roads lined by a series of cyst tombs, probably destined to the middle class (also including foreign Greek and Italic individuals) made up of merchants and businessmen. A plan based on the social hierarchy of the dead must therefore already have existed in the necropolis of the VI century. The Tomb of the Bronze Figurine of an Offering-bearer was built using regular-shaped panchina blocks, dry-walled using a perfected technique of assembling the elements by means of inserting wooden hinges between the quoins, as can be deduced from other collapsed tombs of the same type with cylindrical housings inside the blocks.

Oriented westward, the building has no foundations and rests on a slightly larger base. The square-plan cell is surmounted by a roof with two slopes, made by means of a double order of panchina slabs: a first series of four larger slabs forms the ceiling, while smaller elements form the outer covering. The presence of a housing hole in one of the panchina roof slabs and stone fragments found in the vicinity of the tomb, has enabled reconstructing a complex decorative structure that adorned the top of the building, with lithic sculptures and akroteria (terracotta or stone elements used to decorate the roofs of buildings). Other examples of this tomb typology are the Tomb of the Attic Cups and the three tombs of the Sughera della Capra of which only the bases remain.

also had a small cell where a cinerary urn was entombed.

Walking towards the sea, we come to a small basin: these are the lands of the old Casone farm. Here, scoria formed a layer about ten meters thick, covering every stone of the necropolis.

For this very reason, the **Tomb of the Strainers** has come to us intact: scoria weight did not break the slabs of alberese used to make the dome, nor did looters of

Small model of the Tomb of the Bronze Figurine of an Offering-bearer (second half VI century - first half V century BC) with the reconstruction of the roof decoration on the basis of fragments found.

any epoch ever discover its existence. The stone that sealed the tomb still stands beside the entrance. The tomb was only discovered in 1960 when the removal of iron residues had by then already terminated. The skeletons still rested inside the chamber. The family of the dead loved ritual banquets: the tomb contained iron skewers for roasting and two strainers for straining wine sweetened with fruit, honey and spices.

The Casone area also has several simple **sarcophagus tombs**. Was this perhaps the

The aediculum tomb of the Bronze Figurine of an Offering-bearer (late VI - early V century BC) in the Necropolis of Casone.

cemetery of the poor? In reality, this corner of the burial ground was destined to hold the graves of the middle class Populonians. Iron craftsmen could not afford the funeral pomp of the city's rich merchants or the owners of the first forges but they still wanted to be buried under the same hill. The more humble were buried in fossa tombs. The tombs of this small necropolis are aligned with the more elegant aediculum tombs: a road

Sarcophagus Tombs

This burial typology appeared in Populonia in the course of the VI century BC and was probably destined to a middle class (formed principally by foreigners such as Greeks and Italic peoples) that handled the practical management of the trade and manufacturing activities in the district of Populonia.

A sarcophagus tomb is formed by a stone parallelepiped-shaped case of varying dimensions and a lithic cover which could assume different configurations. The burial case could be made following different techniques: a single block, hollowed out in the middle or two blocks hollowed out and perfectly aligned; this type of tomb was generally completed by a monolithic slab with a semicircular shape or ridged to form a cover. At times, the tomb instead consisted of a stone slab laid out horizontally and four more slabs connected to form the walls of the case. The cover of the latter typology generally consisted of two lithic slabs to form a sloping roof and a fillet hiding the point of connection between the two elements.

Small bronze statue portraying the image of a male worshipper in the act of making an offering to a divinity (V century BC). It probably formed the top of a candelabrum and was found in the Tomb of the Bronze Figurine of an Offering-bearer, hence its name.

probably passed by this cemetery. Several tomb covers, almost always stone monoliths, reproduced sloping roofs and, by means of holes, were soldered with lead to the walls of the "coffin."

A curious archaeological enigma: one of the sarcophagi is sculpted in nenfro stone (a kind of sandstone), a material unknown in the quarries of Populonia but well known in the lands of Vulci.

The dead person was certainly an important figure and from a rich family: the expense of transporting such a monolith from inland Etruria was no joking matter.

Equally rich and powerful must also have been the family that built the little aediculum temple known as the **Tomb of the Bronze Figurine of an Offering-bearer**. This was one of the last tombs to reappear from beneath the layer of scoria that covered Casone: in one of the most famous photographs of the rediscovery of Populonia, we note a corner of the

Tall Tumulus Tombs

Tomb of the Strainers

This type of construction, called "Tall Tumulus Tombs," does not have the panchina drum that characterizes the tombs with crepidoma (base), like the Tomb of the Chariots or that of the Funeral Couches: the tumulus is set on the same level as the cell, lined with a layer of clay to make it impermeable and surrounded by a series of stone slabs that define its circumference.
The short entrance corridor (*dromos*), delimited on the sides by two walls of alberese stone, is not covered and was generally obstructed with stones. To either side of the central aisle were the spaces for laying out the dead, delimited by two slabs of alberese placed edgeways, while the funeral goods were presumably set inside the cell's central aisle.
In 1960, in the course of agricultural earthmoving following scoria removal, one of these tombs was found intact. It can be dated to the end of the VII century BC (though its reuse during the Hellenistic Age, towards the late IV and early III centuries BC, appears certain): the so-called tomb of the Strainers.

sepulcher emerging from the hill of iron residues. This tomb stood up to the weight of the scoria very well which, indeed, measured more than seven meters. Utilized between the VI and IV centuries BC and violated in Etruscan times, this tomb is beautiful: a true funeral temple, the only one in Populonia of aediculum architecture that has come down to us.
Many of the almost baroque decorative friezes have been lost: the roof was enhanced by fantasy animals and small sculptures with whirls and spirals. The tomb raiders probably did not see the little statue that decorated a candelabrum.
A very fascinating object whose interpretation is object of much controversy: one of the man's arms is raised while the other supports a vase or disk. Is he a discus-thrower or a worshipper in the act of making an offering? Just one more curious interrogative posed by the Necropolis of Casone.

Via del Ferro

"The Via del Ferro" climbs up the hill of Poggio della Porcareccia, proceeds around Conchino and then connects with the Via delle Cave itinerary. The Via del Ferro crosses through the ancient industrial settlements of Populonia and reaches the tomb of the Italo-Corinthian Fragments in the woods. It penetrates deep into the forest of oak and cork trees, typical vegetation of the Piombino promontory. Time needed: 2 hours. The itinerary is indicated by blue signs.

Populonia was a frenetic city that moved to a fast rhythm, a city of workmen and merchants. Here, iron was in command, along with the fires that heated Elban hematite, the breathtaking heat of forges. On every site of the Etruscan adventure, the necropolises have left us precious traces and indispensable clues to unveil the mysteries of this people, but Populonia, like every industrial city, was a center of life, business, trade and transactions. The Via del Ferro is today a tranquil path, a nature trail that climbs up through woods of cork and oak trees, but if you just look at the soles of your shoes, you will find fragments of hematite and residues, more than two thousand five hundred years old, of the scoria abandoned by the Etruscans. Don't be fooled by today's pleasant landscape: the Via del Ferro was a tumultuous road that ran between industrial buildings and forges constantly burning. Here slept the workmen of these ancient ironworks, here stood craftsmen's shops, here merchants sought semi-finished products to sell to their customers.

The Via del Ferro itinerary slips behind the Botanical Garden and climbs up Poggio della Porcareccia. We then detour left to observe a large circular tomb. This is the tomb of the Amber Beads, built in the VII century BC, and excavated between 1924 and 1925.
The mule track climbs up the hill of Porcareccia and approaches the ruins of an authentic district. This is the double complex of the **Industrial Buildings**, among the

most precious testimonies of Populonia's metalworking activity, where in the VI century BC stood one of the working class quarters of town. A craftsmen's area, built outside the city walls. Here there was water and a ventilated microclimate. Here, the smelters and blacksmiths of antiquity, along with the immigrants in search of work in Populonia, worked, lived, slept and spent their day. The in-

dustrial area must have covered a vast area: it certainly reached the locality today known as **Campo Sei**, extended over the slopes of Poggio della Porcareccia and grazed the walls of the city's residential area. Life in the working class quarter was convulsive: several times it was rebuilt and increased by new buildings, while others were knocked down, until its final destruction in the early III century BC.

On the hill of Porcareccia, we also find other tombs: the **Tomb of the Fans** was found intact in 1927. It dates to the VII century BC and miraculously survived

The drum of the chamber Tomb of the Bronze Fans (mid VII - mid VI century BC) on Poggio della Porcareccia, made of blocks of panchina stone. The picture shows one of the two limestone stele that stand at the *dromos* entrance.

The Industrial Quarter of Porcareccia

The "industrial" area of the Poggio della Porcareccia, where the metallurgical and manufacturing activities of Populonia were conducted, is located outside the circle of walls that enclosed the lower city, in an area used as a necropolis until the third-quarter of the VI century. The set-tlement dates to the second half of the same century and was formed by workshops and dwellings of iron workmen. A road, probably from the Hellenistic epoch, connected the quarter with the upper city, the acropolis: traces of it remain south of the industrial buildings, on the Poggio della Porcareccia. Excavation campaigns brought to light several constructions which, situated on a bank of natural clay, housed several rudimentary forges that were found full of iron scoria and pipe fragments.

An interpretation of excavation data seems to aver the hypothesis that the forges for reducing the iron mineral are prior to the build-ings, erected around 540-530 BC. Archaeological studies have evidenced various phases in the use of the constructions up until the early III century BC, as testified by a series of beaten clay floors, stratified and planted on different layers of scoria deposits (with a honeycomb function). The side-walls are made of regular dry-walled blocks and the rooms in antiquity were covered with a red plaster made from a mixture of lime and sand. Below floor level in several rooms, a system of water conduits was found which, through openings in the side-walls, seems to have conveyed waste waters to an external ditch. Probably built in the III century BC, a furnace with grating, supported by a

The "industrial" buildings on Poggio della Porcareccia. Detail of the wall bond.

Etruscan workmen who, more than two centuries later, burnt iron ores in a forge that stood nearby. This grave escaped their notice and was thus not looted. This was indeed fortunate: inside the tomb, archaeologists found three stupendous bronze fans of amazing beauty, known as the "Flabelli."

The Tomb of the Goldwork, famous for its very rich funeral goods, was discovered in 1940 on the eve of World War II. A splendid moon-shaped razor, modeled in bronze, was found in the burial chamber. Someone had already attempted to

terracotta pilaster of a type very similar to those found in the settlement of Madonna di Fucinaia near Campiglia Marittima, was found outside the buildings. The opinions on the use of this type of forge are still discordant: proposals include the function of roasting minerals (before the reduction process) or that of firing ceramics, but also for working bronze in crucibles. The finding of a tun full of ashes, charcoal and bones could make one think of the preparatory operations for obtaining the clay destined to line the furnaces or to make crucibles: in this case, the building could be interpreted, in this phase, as a warehouse for materials. From the inscriptions in Etruscan discovered on several ceramic fragments found during excavations and indicating the name of the object's owner, it seems likely that some of the workmen employed in metallurgical activities were foreign and of low class. The structures studied certainly represent only a very small part of what the entire industrial quarter must have been. The settlement probably developed to the point of including "Campo Sei," closer to the residential settlement but much more compromised by the modern interventions of scoria recovery that have left evident testimony even in the very name of the place.

Global view of the "industrial quarter" of Porcareccia. The buildings date to the second half of the VI century BC but were used in different phases, as can be educed from the stratification of different floorings in beaten clay.

violate the tombs of the **Golden Hair-spring** and of the **Aryballoi** (small containers for perfumed oils): their failure permitted archaeologists in 1932 to discover precious women's tomb goods. These two tombs had a unique destiny: after their discovery, they were again covered with iron scoria and only uncovered again in 1956.

The mule track of the Via del Ferro enters the woods of oak and cork, a recent forest, though dense and pleasant. Amidst the trees, watchful eyes will note traces of the ancient and modern history of Populonia: almost everywhere you will see segments of thick walls, strange depressions of the ground, ditches made to recover scoria. Every rock in this area hides fragments of an Etruscan or Roman story. Or it is simply the memory of the colossal activity of recovering iron scoria in the course of this century. Or perhaps they are ditches where votive objects of abandoned sanctuaries were thrown. Only someone who has spent years searching these woods could show you where a pavement was excavated or where houses and workshops are thought to have stood.

In the middle of the woods, there suddenly emerges the large Tomb of the Italo-Corinthian Fragments. Only the Tomb of the Chariots in the lower necropolis of San Cerbone is larger than this one with

Traveling the Via del Ferro, we come to the Industrial Buildings.

The chamber Tomb of the Italo-Corinthian Fragments in the locality of Conchino, along the Via del Ferro itinerary.

its sixteen meter circumference. Excavated in 1954, it dates to the VII century BC but its treasure had already been violated by ancient grave-robbers: its interior contained only fragments of vases for unguents that craftsmen of southern Etruria had modeled, imitating the Corinthian styles.

The excavation campaigns conducted between 1997 and 1998 revealed three more tombs positioned on the same line as the tomb of the Italo-Corinthian Fragments, giving rise to a suggestive hypothesis: did a road come by this necropolis? It was probably one that connected the port and the districts that stood on the Poggio della Guardiola.

The Via del Ferro passes round the hill of Conchino. Retaining stairs have been modeled in the ground by entwining tree branches: a very ancient technique. The track around Conchino can lead to the Tombs of the Aryballoi and the Tomb of the Golden Hairspring and, then to the Visitors Center. A connecting path instead joins the Via del Ferro to the Campo all'Arpia meadow, the Experimental Archaeology Workshop and the Via delle Cave route.

Via delle Cave

*The "Way of Quarries" climbs up through the highest part of the Archaeological Park, past the meadow of Campo dell'Arpia and crosses a lovely forest of cork and oak trees. It goes in search of the ancient Etruscan quarries that excavated the walls of rock, stripping them of the panchina stone used to build the city of Populonia and her necropolises. In the Hellenistic years (IV-III centuries BC), the quarries were used as new burial grounds: new underground chamber tombs (*hypogea*) were dug deep in the rock. Recent excavations by archaeologists have uncovered an impressive complex of 33 underground chamber tombs. A splendid lookout commands a view of the Le Grotte quarry pit and a moving panorama of the Gulf of Baratti and the Val di Cornia. Excursion time: 2 hours. A series of red signs indicates the itinerary. The beginning of the Via delle Cave is marked by a rest area with bathroom facilities and the experimental archaeology workshop shelter.*

Campo dell'Arpia is a meadow that stretches out towards Selva di Baratti, the forest that covers the hills of Populonia. The little road that climbs up towards the Via delle Cave runs along this field which was cultivated until recent times. This meadow concealed part of the VII and VI century necropolis. The industrial Populonia of the IV-III centuries BC built a craftsmen's center over these tombs and heaped iron scoria which, at that time, was useless.

In the fifties, the excavators of mining companies violently assailed Campo dell'Arpia, leveling the terrain, flattening it, digging a chasm thirty meters deep to recover the iron slag abandoned by the Etruscans. Few were the ruins that survived the mechanical shovels and the incursions of grave-robbers. In 1950, an earth-mover of the "Populonia Italica" company ran into the corner of a tomb, shattering the vault and making the walls collapse. From the tomb emerged a fragment of a candelabrum: the little bronze statue portraying a harpy, the bird-monster of Greek mythology. During excavations in 1997, Campo dell'Arpia yielded

A sign marks the Via delle Cave itinerary.

another cyst tomb with bucchero fragments, the characteristic black ceramics of the Etruscans.

At the end of Campo dell'Arpia, past the rest area, begins Selva di Baratti, a wood of holm oak, and the Via delle Cave itinerary. For decades, this was one of the less explored archaeological areas of Populonia. As well as one of the most fascinating. Large walls of ivory-colored rock appear amidst the holm oaks of this

An ancient panchina quarry inside a holm oak wood. You can still see the signs left by the stone-cutters in working the material.

hill: here the Etruscan stone-cutters extracted the stone necessary for their constructions. These are quarries of panchina stone, a calcareous sandstone (known as calcarenite), that is easy to work and forms especially along the Tyrrheanian coasts. Panchina is abundant in the heights of Populonia and the stone-cutters of antiquity successfully exploited the deposits of Le Grotte and Buche delle Fate. The Etruscans extracted almost 34,000 cubic meters of panchina from these quarries. Once abandoned, the quarries were used as necropolises when the industrial city expanded beyond all

"Panchina" a building stone

A calcareous-arena-ceous stone (cal-carenite), formed by sandy sediments, rich in cemented organic fragments. It generally originates on the beaches of the Tyrrheanian coast where there are sources of lime but can also be formed following the action of wind. A formation of this type is the one that accumulated in the two paleo-valleys on the two opposite slopes of the water-shed of Poggio della Guardiola and Poggio Pecorino, today traversed by the channels of Le Grotte and Le Fate. During the glacial phases, when the level of the sea had diminished and the promontory of Populonia was sur-rounded by great ex-panses of sand, the wind carried the sands which de-posited in the two valleys, giving rise to the formations of panchina at Le Grotte and Buche delle Fate.

forecasts: it was not difficult to drill panchina and the Etruscans dug deep subterranean tombs.

Quarries and tombs are immediately vis-ible to anyone who climbs up to the woods of Le Grotte. A wall, practically covered with ivy, forms the backdrop of the landscape past a wood of holm oak: this was the quarry of the Protome. Square-shaped rubble lies on the ground: fragments unused by the Etruscan stone-cutters. Three tombs are lined up beside the quarry: steep moss-covered steps lead to the hypogeum. This solitary necropolis immediately attracted the at-tention of grave-robbers who did not hesitate to violate the graves. They also sought to chisel off and carry away a cu-rious and surprising decoration that hung in the vault of the **Tomb of the Protome** (protomes are the decorative elements which, in the art of antiquity, portrayed a human or animal head). It is the only trace of sculpture that appears in the tombs of Populonia: a roughly modeled

Traces of working the panchina walls in the Hellenistic necropolis of Le Grotte inside the an-cient quarry.

female head, left unfinished by an unknown sculptor. On rainy days, water slowly drips off the nose of this figure that remained buried for more than two thousand years. Ceramic fragments found in the tomb attest that this small necropolis was used from the IV to the II centuries BC.

The footpath does not reach the crest of Poggio Pecorino and, before the ridge, bends towards the sea and dips into the basin of **Cava Piccola**. Here, the wall of panchina is a semicircle that clearly shows the traces of Etruscan excavation assays. Suddenly, an embrasure opens among the trees: the **Lookout** of the Archaeological Park is like a balcony facing a beautiful panorama. It is an authentic surprise: the Lookout was cut out on the highest side of the pit of the vast **Cava delle Grotte**, one of the main quarries in the hills of Populonia, sheer over one of the extraction walls. From this point, you can admire the wall sculpted by stone-cutters of the VII and VI centuries BC: like a little fortified castle with amber-colored walls, immersed in a dense wood. The Etruscans of the Hellenistic centuries (IV-III centuries BC) drilled the rocky walls and dug the graves of a new necropolis: Populonia was by now a rich and very populated city that needed new cemeteries. It was easy to cut the chambers into the panchina and there bury the dead. Already opened and looted in Roman times, the Le Grotte necropolis area was several times violated by grave-robbers from Piombino: a first excavation campaign was organized in 1979 and, finally, between 1997 and 1998, the entire area was studied in depth.

Leaving the Lookout, the path descends to the quarry pit and the meeting point for guided visits. The quarry area is exceptional: you can almost hear the stone-cutters strike the stone or the rock that rumbles before breaking into blocks under the pressure of the wedges. The quarry wall that rises opposite the necropolis "castle" is a slope of sculpted stone, an abandoned field of cultivation. You can

The Quarries

The mining basin of Le Grotte is located on the south-eastern slope of Poggio della Guardiola, between 80 and 140 meters above sea level. The areas recognized as ancient panchina quarries, till today, number four, apparently exploited at least from the VII century BC, as demonstrated by the blocks of this material utilized in the construction of the tumulus tombs of San Cerbone. Panchina was extracted following the natural layers of rock sedimentation. Two types of procedures were used: excavating by steps, which is to say, working on different levels of the bed, with the advantage of operating in different points of the work site at the same time, and following a "grid" system whereby it was possible to work two contiguous blocks. Traces of both of these mining procedures were found at Le Grotte on the slope forming the quarry bed abandoned in the course of work. The ditches were dug using a pickaxe and then made deeper using iron wedges. This was one of the most difficult and delicate operations and therefore, in more ancient times, natural cracks in the rock were sought and mechanical levers of poles were used or holes were chiseled into the base of the blocks. In more remote times, the wedges, probably made of wood, were made to swell with water and break the material. The blocks extracted were of rather small dimensions and close to those necessary for use in constructions. An analysis of the traces found on the quarrying surface evidenced measurements in which one of the three dimensions is greater than one meter, while the other two are smaller. Block extraction was probably performed by small teams of specialized stone-cutters. The operation of shaping and smoothing the stone blocks and columns was probably performed inside the extraction area, as the finished elements ready for use and found in the area, would seem to demonstrate.

Reconstruction of stone-cutters' activity in the area of Le Grotte that can be visited. On a sloping mining floor, abandoned in the course of work, the blocks were cut vertically on four sides and then separated from the quarry bed by means of wedges.

clearly see the cuts made by the Etruscan stone-cutter: the block of panchina was almost detached from the wall by opening four vertical cracks in which wedges were inserted. After hours of delivering blows and with great fatigue, the rough

stone finally detached from the quarry bed. Before being transported d o w n h i l l, t h e squared mass was probably worked i n s i d e t h e p i t, equipped with a small workshop. A small isolated sarcophagus tomb (III century BC) is at the center of the quarry.

The necropolis of Le Grotte quarry is like a cemetery on several layers. In the sixties and seventies, almost all of the tombs were sacked by grave-robbers from Piombino: you can still note the tunnel they dug in a corner of the quarry to reach the first level of the necropolis and break into the row of tombs. The horizontal tunnel dug by grave-robbers grazes two chamber tombs. Only Tomb 14, the lowest, escaped their attention and was discovered inviolate in 1997: the funeral goods of a cremated woman were found intact. It dates to the IV-III century BC and is on show in the Visitors Center. The doors of the tombs, like windows, look out over the quarry pit. Experts can show you otherwise invisible writing on the rocky wall opposite: a small circle seems to enclose the number 150. Was it quarrying information for the Etruscan workmen? A few meters away, lettering from right to left: can you read the name Annas? Or is it Anas? Archaeologists hypothesize that it identifies the owner of the tomb below.

A curious fact: on the left corner of the necropolis-quarry, a sort of large cube (the symbol of the signs indicating the meeting points) has been cut into the

The chamber tombs of the Hellenistic necropolis of Le Grotte (IV-II centuries BC). Preceded by a downward sloping *dromos* and built with steps, it contained two or three dead persons, laid out on beds made in the rock.

Reconstruction of a series of underground chamber tombs of the Hellenistic Age.

The access *dromos* to one of the tombs of the Hellenistic Age, dug into the panchina.

The Underground Chamber Tombs of the Hellenistic Age

The underground chamber tomb (*hypogeum*) typology, dug into marl, clay or panchina, spread to Populonia during the Hellenistic period (IV-III centuries BC). In Populonia, they were frequently distributed in rows, dug into outcrops or arranged along the walls of ancient abandoned panchina quarries, at times reaching great depths. The tombs could be preceded by an uncovered corridor (*dromos*), dug into the rock, often with steps down to the entrance, generally set at a greater depth than the surrounding land.

A room leading to the cell was at times arch-shaped above and closed by one or more slabs of panchina lodged in specially made cavities. Following each burial, the *dromos* was obstructed by means of filling it with earth and stones; the generally rectangular-plan cell was dug into the panchina and had a flat or slightly arched ceiling. The interiors of several tombs still clearly show the traces of the tools used by the ancients to finish the walls ("gravering"). The funeral beds (usually three) are arranged along the sides of the chamber; here, the bodies of the dead or cinerary urns were placed. During the Hellenistic period in fact, the funeral rites of burial and cremation coexisted. At times, rock formations are found on the funeral beds that imitate the pillows on royal beds.

At the necropolis of Le Grotte, the only two frescoed tombs of Populonia were found (the so-called "Corridietro" Tomb and the Tomb of the "Dolphins"), with very simple decorative motifs (waves in motion, dolphins, profiles of funeral beds...), comparable to types found in Cerveteri. Other examples of underground chamber tombs in Etruscan civilization are widespread in many centers of southern Etruria such as Sovana, Blera, Norchia and Castel d'Asso, where grave complexes dug into tufa form the so-called rupestrian necropolises.

rock. This is something of a mystery: how was it possible to cut so deep around the cube? And how would they have ever managed to extract it, if this were really the intention?

A layer of debris, residues of Etruscan stone-working, probably still does cover the true quarry bed: below the level of the last tomb, there remain some eight meters to explore.

Here, beneath meters of filling material, seven fossa tombs were discovered: one grave held the remains of a man, destined to become eternal as the "Etruscan of Tomb E." He was between 1.65 and 1.72 meters tall, of robust build and with the left arm a couple of centimeters shorter than the other, due to a trauma in bringing him to light. As a child he had suffered periods of malnutrition. The man died around 40 years of age from a bone tumor. His teeth were corroded and worn: did he chew animal hides to soften them? Whatever the cause, he was afflicted with annoying infections of the nose and jaw. He consumed a lot of meat and was not too fond of grains. Researchers and computer technicians have managed to reconstruct the body virtually of this Etruscan buried in the stone of Populonia two thousand four hundred years ago.

Climbing back up the hill from the quarry we come to a large complex of underground chamber tombs (almost all violated by grave-robbers and uncovered by excavations conducted between 1967 and 1979) dug into the rock, down steep stairs. This is the Le Grotte necropolis that conceals the Painted Tombs, the only two graves frescoed by the Etruscans of Populonia. They are light, faded, simple drawings: the crest of a wave runs along the wall of the burial chamber while playing dolphins or a ram's strength accompany the dead in his afterworld voyage.

The corridors dug into the earth to reach the sepulchers were often adorned with small statues: lions and protective

Necropolis of Le Grotte: access to a recently excavated tomb whose grave goods are on show at the Visitors Center of San Cerbone.

The *dromos* and entrance to a hypogeum, made in Hellenistic times.

Necropolis of the Coterminous Tombs, dug into the panchina stone in the Hellenistic period.

The "cube" dug into the wall of the ancient Le Grotte quarry.

demons of death whose task it was to watch over the dead. Etruscan workmen did not finish one of the tombs of this small necropolis: they had only managed to cut out the steps leading to the chamber before work was interrupted.

The ceramics that escaped the grave-robbers' notice reveal that this necropolis was used between the IV and II centuries BC.

A short distance ahead, down the path that closes the ring of the Via delle Cave, we come to six more graves: the Coterminous Tombs. Several little archaeological interrogatives have sprung up around this necropolis: Tomb 6 is not aligned with the other graves and is oriented north-south instead of north-east. Moreover: it does not have an access corridor. At the entrance of Tomb 4, vases, plates, jugs and even food remains were found: did the relatives of the dead man celebrate a ritual banquet right in the corridor that led to the sepulcher? The chambers of all the Coterminous Tombs were violated by grave-robbers and it was possible to recover only fragments of worked stone. This necropolis too, was used between the IV and II centuries BC.

A brief walk and we are back to the little main road of the Via delle Cave and the meadow of Campo dell'Arpia.

The promontory of
Populonia with a
glimpse of Elba Island
on the horizon.

Natural Aspects of the Piombino Promontory

The Territory's Evolution

The geological history of the territory of Piombino is tied to the sea and thus to the variations of its level, occurring in the course of the last geological periods. The promontory and little islands of Palmaiola and Cerboli constitute the highest portion of a mountain peninsula which, already in the Tertiary period, included today's Elba Island.

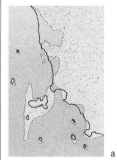

During the Pliocene, about 5 million years ago, the progressive return of the sea, caused by the opening of the strait of Gibraltar, transformed this peninsula and many other elevations of the present Tuscany, into islands. Thus the "Tuscan Paleo-archipelago" was formed by a series of islands scattered in front of the coast and formed by the hills of Montalbano and Chianti.

About 2.5 million years ago, in the mid-upper Pliocene, most of the islands of the Paleo-archipelago were joined to the continent. Successively, in the Quaternary period (lower Pleistocene), about 1,700,000 years ago, the Piombino promontory was already connected to Elba Island and remained separated from the continent by a narrow stretch of sea. In the upper Pleistocene epoch (about 150,000 years ago), the sea divided the promontory from Elba.

During the greatest expansion of polar glaciers and mountains, which occurred some 20,000 years go in the course of the last glaciations, the sea level diminished about 100 meters compared to today and thus substantially modified the geography of all coastal areas in the Mediterranean. In this period, broad plains stretched around the Elba-Piombino mountain ridge, while cold violent winds accumulated sand on hill slopes. At the end of the glaciations, about 10,000 years ago, the sea began to rise again, invading the lower areas of the mountain ridge and transforming Elba again into an island, while the Piombino area, priorly connected to the continent in the north (between Poggio San Leonardo and the Campiglia Hills) became a promontory.

A second sandy ridge joining the southern part of the promontory to the continent, began to form at the end of the Pleistocene as a result of wave motion, giving rise to a far-reaching lagoon, the northern tip of which extended to Poggio all'Agnello and Venturina. Due to a very slow natural process, this water body progressively became a swamp which was filled and reclaimed only in the course of the eighteen-hundreds by means of deviating the course of the Cornia river and creating a network of brooks.

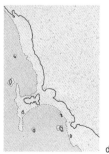

Geology

The backbone of the Piombino promontory is formed by arenaceous rock alternated with layers of silt and shale clays, attributed to the formation of the arenaceous Flysch, known as "Macigno" (calcareous limestone). The term is used to indicate a sandstone with a fine to medium grain, with a limey or lime-clay cement, widespread in the Apennine area. This rock belongs to an Oligocene clayey-limey formation that formed following turbid underground currents, during the orogenetic movement of the Tertiary period. The term Flysch, used with the adjective arenaceous to indicate the "Macigno," is a term of the German Swiss dialect which means "sliding land."

Calcareous limestone is used as a building stone in its *pietra serena* and *pietra forte* varieties which are well-known in Tuscany and were once used to make millstones.

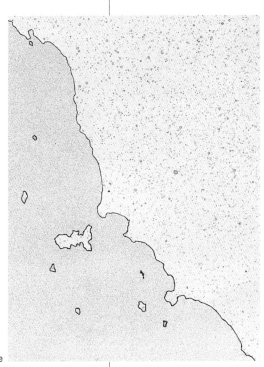

On this formation emerge several areas of silty clays, marls, marley limes and calcarenites of the "Formation of Canetolo" that dates to the Eocene period. The Complex of the Facies Ligure Formations is represented by basalts, that make up practically all of the Falcone peninsula and the small outcrop below Rocchetta, and by argillites and the "Palombini" siliceous limes of Cala Moresca.

Basalts are formed by particular types of lava that emerge in the sea depths, are greenish in color and have a characteristic round shape due to their rapid cooling in water. The basalts of the Piombino promontory originated on the Ligurian ocean floor some 165-185 million years ago and were transported to this area, following intense tectonic movements.

e

a) The coastline during the lower Pleistocene (1,700,000 years ago).

b) Middle Pleistocene (750,000 years ago).

c) Upper Pleistocene (150,000 years ago).

d) Upper Pleistocene (10,000 years ago).

e) The territory's conformation today.

The formation of argillites and "Palombini" siliceous limes consists of alternating layers of grayish-brown colored shale clays and layers of siliceous limes of a gray color, like the feathers of ringdoves, hence the term "Palombini." These clayey and siliceous-lime sediments deposited about 130 million years ago on the floor of the Ligurian ocean, following subterranean landslides.

The promontory gently connects to the plain by means of sandy sediments of the Quaternary period, formed by sandy calcarenites, such as panchina (see box text under the quarry itinerary), and orangey-red sand of Donoratico which rises to become hills and penetrates into the valleys without giving rise to flat or terraced surfaces.

Landscape and Vegetation

The Piombino promontory is covered with a fairly homogenous vegetation of predominantly Mediterranean
woodland, but at the same time conserves important testimonies of species and plant consortiums, characteristic of
climatic situations different from that of today.

The rocky coast has been colonized within a few meters
of the sea by chrithinum and rupestrian *statici* and higher
up by maritime cineraria, wild carrot, helichrysum and
silvery bushes of houseleek; further inland we have
juniper and, fi-
nally, evergreen
shrub. There is
also an interest-
ing presence of
fanpalm which
here has its
northernmost
station in Italy.
Mediterranean
macchia is this
territory's most
representative
flora formation:
it is formed
by plants which,
having to sup-
port hot and arid
summers, have
developed small,

Panoramic view of the
Gulf of Baratti.

thick and coriaceous leaves, in order to reduce water loss
due to transpiration. These evergreen plants are dormant
in the summer period in order to save their energies, while
vegetative activity is relegated to the rest of the year.

The capacity of the macchia plants to produce shoots after cutting has been exploited by man since prehistoric
times and, in particular, by the Etruscans who here found
the wood to burn in forges. The great quantity of scoria
found in the park area testifies to the intense and pro-
longed exploitation of this resource.

The procedures of cutting, burning and grazing, practiced
even today, have influenced this flora formation which today presents successive stages of degeneration and regen-
eration: it is possible to identify the biocenoses (communities of vegetal species that live in a certain station) of
steppe, garigue and low macchia.

The steppe is here represented by the dominant species of
diss, while the garigue is characterized by communities of

low shrubs of mostly aromatic plants such as *stecade*, *santoreggia* and oregano, interspersed with outcrops. The low macchia is formed by shrubs and fruit-bearing bushes that can reach two meters in height, such as the cystus, myrtle, lenticus and brooms. The high macchia is prevalently composed of evergreen shrubs such as lenticus, phillyrea, Italian buckthorn, strawberry-tree, heather, myrtle and viburnum tinus, that grow beneath a wood made up mostly of holm oak, plus cork, manna ash, pubescent oak and the rare domestic sorb. This vegetation is entangled with viney plants such as sarsaparilla, rubia

The countryside around the Gulf of Baratti.

tinctoria, ox-berry, clematis and honeysuckle. The underbrush is formed by cyclamen, violas, butcher's-broom and carpets of ivy.

The mixed wood is formed by vegetal consortiums relegated to cool and humid valleys where we also find species of mountain and Atlantic origin such as the chestnut, broom, holly and laurel. Here we also find the wild grapevine, already cultivated in the Etruscan epoch, as Pliny recalls. The very name of Populonia, *Pupluna*, would seem to descend from *Fufluns*, god of agriculture successively tied to Bacchus or to the root-word *puple*, meaning sprout.

An important ecological component also consists in the environments profoundly modified by man, such as clearings and abandoned fields that host a great variety of pioneer, competitive and mostly herbaceous plants such as lupsia galactites, viper's bugloss, black verbascum, thistle, wild endive…

Fauna

The coast of the Piombino promontory is frequented by various seabird species and, in particular, the herring seagull which nests on the little channel islands (Palmaiola and Cerboli). The Mediterranean macchia hosts a fauna composed of medium and small mammals including the wild boar (by now completely supplanted by hybrid races from north-eastern Europe), hedgehog, fox and martens such as the badger, weasel, skunk and stone marten. Typical birds include the blackcap, Sardinian warbler, titmouse and the *fiorancino*, while the most common reptiles are the viper, rat snake and tortoise. The humid environment of the woods favors the presence of amphibians including the common toad and frogs.

Hedges host a great number of small birds such as the wryneck, common wren and goldfinch, while it is not rare in the clearings to spot the buzzard intent on hunting or the colored magpie searching for small invertebrates in the grass.

The Park woods in the direction of Le Grotte Necropolis

Park Plants

HOLM OAK
Quercus ilex L.
Family of the
Cupuliferae

Its generic name *Quercus* derives from the Celtic *quer* = pretty and *cuez* = tree, while *ilex* is the name by which the Romans indicated this tree. A typically Mediterranean plant that loves warm, dry climates and tends to grow into forests (holm-oak woods), at one time existent along the entire Mediterranean strip. This **evergreen** oak tree that can reach 25 meters in height and more than one thousand years of age, has both male and female flowers and its fruit is an acorn (achene). Its **acorns**, which in the past were gathered for pig farming, are the preferred autumn food of many woodland animals such as the wild boar, squirrel, jay and ringdove; man used the acorns of the holm oak to produce flour from which he made "pan di quercia" (oak bread). The Greeks and Romans used the **bark**, rich in tannin, to tan animal hides. The hard and compact wood can be used to make the handles of instruments and farming tools, to build boats and buildings, but also to make underground constructions because it decomposes so slowly. The dense holm oak forests that in antiquity lined our coasts from the sea to the hills were mostly destroyed by the Etruscans to feed their forges.

MYRTLE
Myrtus communis L.
Family of the
Myrtaceae

Myrtle, also called "mortella" or "mortola," is a typically Mediterranean shrub species with long-stalked white and perfumed solitary flowers. Its **fruit** are berries that, when ripe, are bluish-black in color with metallic reflections. Myrtle is among the classic plants that have played such an important part in the legends and history of Mediterranean peoples. It was sacred to the Persians who used it to feed their sacred fires; the Romans consecrated it to Venus as the symbol of love and peace, and still today, it is used at wedding ceremonies as a valid substitute for orange blossom. Crowns of myrtle were worn by magistrates and Olympic game winners, but the Romans introduced the use of garlanding poets and playwrights. The **bark, leaves** and **flowers** produce an oil, known as "eau d'anges" (water of angels), used in perfumery, but it also has medicinal, balsamic and astringent actions. Its berries, the preferred food of many birds, can be fermented to obtain an acidulous beverage or even used to make jam or, as an added ingredient to several liqueurs. The leaves too, are used in spirits (*mirto bianco*).

LENTISCUS
Pistacia lentiscus L.
Family of the
Anacardiaceae

The lentiscus, also known as "sondro," is a shrubby plant with many branches and small alternate ovate-lanceolate leaves with a pronounced resinous smell.
Its **fruit** consists of small reddish-brown drupes that blacken when ripe. Lentiscus is one of the prized plants of Mediterranean macchia for the useful products it supplies man. The **leaves**, rich in tannins, can be used as tanning agents; the squeezed fruit produces a greenish oil that is eatable and can be burned. The **trunk and branches**, when tapped, give off a pleasant-smelling resin, known since antiquity as "Chio mastic" (from the name of the Greek island), used in eastern Mediterranean countries as a masticator to strengthen the gums and scent the breath (the first chewing-gum). This plant can also be used as a graft for the pistachio (*Pistacia vera*).

STRAWBERRY-TREE
Arbustus unedo L.
Family of the
Ericaceae

The strawberry-tree, also known as "albatro" in Italian, has large shiny dentate-lanceolate **leaves**; the flowers, spotless white with a corolla shaped like a wineskin, hang in slightly pendulous groups. The eatable **fruit** is made up of round berries recalling the strawberry; though attractive to the eye, they have little taste, many small seeds and a tough skin. The very etymology of the scientific name, unedo or unum edo = "I shall have only one," reveals this fruit's scarce qualities as a food. Be that as it may, they are picked and used to make jams (with astringent properties) and a type of brandy. In folk medicine, a decoction of strawberry-tree leaves was widely used to regulate the intestine, as a urinary antiseptic and anti-rheumatic. In Greece, the wood is usually used to make flutes.

CORK
Quercus suber L.
Family of the
Cupuliferae

The cork tree is an evergreen oak like the holm oak, the bark of which produces a particular quality of cork, known to man for more than two thousand years. Cork is light, it floats, does not transmit heat, is impermeable to liquids and stands up brilliantly to fire; indeed, the cork tree is unlikely to die in forest fires. The Romans used cork to make comfortable sandals and floats for the

fishing nets, but it was only with the XV century, with the large-scale production of glass bottles, that cork forests began to be rationally exploited. Today, use of the cork tree is regulated by law; the tree survives the periodic stripping of its bark as long as the live tissues immediately beneath are not damaged.

LAUREL
Laurus nobilis L.
Family of the
Lauraceae

The laurel has hard and aromatic lanceolate leaves, dark green in color, and reaches heights of more than ten meters. Its fruit consists of large, oval, green drupes which in October, when ripe, become black. Venerated since antiquity, the Greeks considered it sacred to Apollo and its flexible branches, entwined to make crowns and garlands, were considered symbols of success, virtue and glory. Warriors and poets, among both the Greeks and Romans, were crowned with laurel garlands. The word "baccolaureato" refers to the berries of the laurel

and the garlands that rested on the heads of scholars and poets when they received academic honors. The **leaves** are used in cooking to season meats, as well as in decoctions to stimulate gastric secretion, alleviate menstruation or as a sudorific and carminative (that favors the expulsion of intestinal gas). The drupes, rich in oily essence, fats and tannin, are used as stimulants in baths but especially for the so-called laurel oil or butter which is used, along with other substances, in making "laurel unguent," a folk medicine to fight rheumatism and gout.

HAWTHORN
Crataegus monogyna Jacq.
Family of the *Rosaceae*

In April-May hawthorn ("albaspina" for the ancient Romans) explodes with a great mass of very fragrant flowers, similar to small roses, which in part conceal the young leaves. In Autumn, its abundant red fruit, insipid to human taste, ripens with the cold and supplies a much loved food to sparrows and blackbirds.

The Greeks considered this plant emblem of hope and used it in their religious-nuptial processions to adorn the altars of the goddess Hymen. In the Middle Ages, its symbolism changed. Indeed, it was even said that the thorny branches of the hawthorn were used to make Christ's crown. The plant in Germany was called "Cristdorn" which means thorn of Christ. In herbal medicine, hawthorn is known for its calming, antispasmodic properties and its action against heart disease.

WILD GRAPEVINE
Vitis sylvestris.
Family of the *Vitaceae*

The wild grapevine is a woody, creeping plant with ramified tendrils, profoundly lobate and palmate **leaves**. A form of grapevine was already present in our woods during the Quaternary period. The **fruit** of this plant was used all through prehistory, though its cultivation dates only to the Iron Age. It appears that actual viticulture originated in Sicily two thousand years before Christ. Successively, it was perhaps the Etruscans to cultivate the grapevine and spread it to the rest of the peninsula. The Romans then contributed to spreading it throughout the Mediterranean. It is not known when the art of winemaking was born, perhaps at the same time as viticulture. In any event, Italy was already known in antiquity for its wine production, indeed called "enotria."

CHICORY
Cichorium intybus.
Family of the
Asteraceae

Chicory (from the Greek *kichèo* = to find and *oros* = hills "because wild, it abounds in the hills,") born in Tuscany as wild radicchio, is a composite plant that in summer, when most summer flowers have withered, explodes in splendid blue **flowers** that last until late Autumn. The buds open in the morning with the sun and close at noon. The Romans called this plant *intybus* = endive, because they used it as uncooked salad. In the XVIII century, chicory was

intensely cultivated for its roots which, when roasted, produced the famous coffee of Prussia, dedicated to Frederick the Great, founder of Prussian military power. This "coffee," also known as "chicory," then became one of the ingredients for "vecchina," a substitute for coffee, produced in Tuscany and widely consumed during World War II. Wild chicory, however, is a plant rich in medicinal properties: excellent depurative of the blood, for its bitter principals and content of potassium nitrate (a virtue known also to Pliny), a good digestive and a mild laxative. It is very useful in all cases of pruritic dermatosis, owing to liver and abdominal ailments. Also excellent for treating pimples and abscesses by means of applying the fresh leaves.

CERRIS
Quercus cerris L.
Family of the
Cupuliferae

The cerris is a deciduous oak (its leaves fall in winter) that can reach impressive dimensions of even up to 40 meters. The **leaves**, deeply indented and lobate,

are long and narrow in shape, while its squat **acorn** is surmounted by a scaly top, almost forming a small hedgehog. Its **wood** was used especially in shipyards. The oak tree has always been the subject of an intense symbolism: sacred to Zeus for the Greeks, symbol of strength, physical and moral vigor for the ancient Romans. It is the tree to which man has always devoted the greatest respect, consecrating it to the most important divinities.

CHESTNUT
Castanea sativa L.
Family of the
Cupuliferae

The chestnut tree, originating in Iran, is a species that easily adapts to the climate of our continent up to an altitude of 800-900 meters above sea level. It can reach 30 meters in height, 15 meters circumference and live for more than 1000 years. The indented-edged **leaves** are large and fall in winter. The **fruit**, the chestnut, is protected by an involucre covered with prickles, called husk, and ripens in the months of October-November. Its name is

the translation of the Latin *castanea* which derives from Castanis, a sea town in Asia Minor, whence the plant was imported through Greece and to Europe. In the woods of Italy, the chestnut tree has always been favored in its development especially for economical reasons: entire towns of the Apennines found sustenance from trading chestnuts, from their derivatives and **wood** for building.

BUCKTHORN
Rhamnus alaternus L.
Family of the
Rhamnaceae

Buckthorn is known as an evergreen shrub with ovate or lanceolate, alternate, whole, shiny **leaves** that reaches 5 meters in height. Very old specimens can reach the dimensions of a tree. It is a dioecious plant: the unisexual flowers without corolla, greenish in color and emitting a bad smell, are grouped in strips. When ripe, the **fruit** is a small red drupe. At one time, the **wood** of the buckthorn, particularly hard, was used to build the cobbler's work tools. Because of its unpleasant odor, its wood was called "stink-wood" in Tuscany.

VIBURNUM
Viburnum tinus L.
Family of the
Caprifoliaceae

Viburnum or "laurustine" is an **evergreen** shrub, from 1 to 3 meters high, with opposing, elliptical, dark-green **leaves**, glossy and hairless above, lighter and somewhat downy below. The **flowers**, white that softens into pink, are joined in an inflorescence (corimbo). The **fruit** consists of small, blackish drupes when ripe. Viburnum is a characteristic presence in Tuscan Mediterranean macchia. This plant is often used for ornamental purposes in city gardens and flower-beds.

BUTCHER'S-BROOM
Ruscus aculeatus L.
Family of the *Liliaceae*

This small **evergreen** shrub tends to form impenetrable masses in the underbrush of Mediterranean macchia. Contrary to what it might first seem, butcher's-broom has no leaves which, instead, are substituted by small, modified and sharp twigs, called "cladodes" that have **flowers** in the middle. Its spiny **fronds** were used to protect salted meats from mice, hence its Italian name "pungitopo." Thanks to its **red berries** and pointy cladodes, butcher's-broom has evoked the same symbolism as holly: it was used as a vegetal amulet to ward off evil. This usage has come down even to present-day and thus, it is not rare to find branches of butcher's-broom on door jambs in the Christmas season. Today, butcher's-broom is protected by law which forbids massive collecting.

HEATHER
Erica arborea L.
Family of the *Ericaceae*

Heather, or "broom," is an **evergreen** bushy shrub with densely downy branches and verticillate, strictly linear **leaves**. Its flowers are minute, white, bell-shaped and joined in dense terminal inflorescences. The fruit consists of small capsules containing many seeds. Heather grows on acidic soil. Tree heather **branches** are used to make brooms, while the **trunk** is cut at the base to make pipes. In the astral calendar of herbs, heather belongs to the sign of Scorpio and allegedly softens the character, attenuates passion and favors more constant and persistent efforts towards one's desired objectives.

PHILLYREA
Phillyrea angustifolia L.
Family of the
Oleaceae

Phillyrea (also "lilatro" in Italian) is an **evergreen** shrub, up to 2.5 meters high with leaves that are opposing, coriaceous, lanceolate and similar to those of the olive-tree, but finely serrated, intense green in color on the upper surface, lighter on the lower surface. The not particularly conspicuous **flowers** are small, white and arranged in racemes. The **fruit** is a drupe, black when ripe, very rich in water. Its **wood** is hard and compact, similar to that of the olive, and once supplied an excellent carbon. In the case of forest fires, the phillyrea can produce many sprouts in little time.

ASH
Fraxinus ornus L.
Family of the
Oleaceae

Manna ash, or ash, is a tree which can reach 20 meters in height. Its leaves are composite, odd-pinnate, with 3-4 pair of opposing leaves; the flowers are grouped into terminal panicles. The fruit has membrane wings to assist transportation by the wind and, in botany, is termed "samara." In Greek, manna ash was called "*melia*," a word with the same root as "*méli*," meaning honey. Indeed, tapping its **bark** produces a viscous, sugary sap which, in the XVI century, was sold by chemists as a mild laxative, a property shared with common ash (*F. excelsior*) from which mannitol is extracted to produce manna sugar. Its wood, fairly prized, is known for its characteristic flexibility and elasticity that make it suited to making bows.

FIELD MAPLE
Acer campestre L.
Family of the *Aceraceae*

The name derives from the Latin *acer* = sharp, referring to the five pointy lobes of the Norway maple (*A. platanoides*). Unlike the other species, the **leaves** of the field maple, which do not turn red before falling in autumn but yellow, are distinguished by their 5 characteristic ribs, arranged in a radial pattern starting from the leaf-stalk. The **fruit** has a membranous wing disposed in couples so as to form a sort of propeller that rotates as it falls to the ground. The **wood** of maples, including the field maple, is suited to making musical instruments: indeed, it is used for the bottom, side strips and neck of

violins. Antonio Stradivari was the first to use it in the XVII century to fashion a bridge to support the strings of the violin.

ELM
Ulmus minor Miller.
Family of the *Ulmaceae*

Often of small dimensions, the field elm contributes to the formation of hedges, along with blackthorn and blackberry. It can easily be distinguished from other trees, especially from the hornbeam that has very similar leaves, for the characteristic asymmetry of its **leaves** compared to the central nervations. Indeed, if we fold an elm leaf along the central rib, the two halves will not perfectly overlap. Several medicinal functions have been attributed to the elm since antiquity, from the coagulant and soothing properties of the leaves applied to

wounds, to the properties of the **roots** to make hair grow again. In effect, the leaves and bark contain tannin, silica and potassium which have cicatrizant, depurative, tonic and astringent properties. In phytotherapy, the bark is used still today, as a tincture or decoction to treat cutaneous eruptions and wounds.

PUBESCENT OAK
Quercus pubescens Will.
Family of the *Fagaceae*

Among deciduous oaks, pubescent oak is the one that best adapts to high temperatures and often lives in association with holm oak. The widely lobate **leaves** are distinguished from those of the cerris for their clearly wider, almost oval shape; it can be easily distinguished from other oaks for the thick whitish down on the young branches that bear the **gems**, protecting them from

the summer Mediterranean heat.

BLACKTHORN
Prunus spinosa L.
Family of the *Rosacee*

Thorny shrub with deciduous **leaves** (they fall during winter), the blackthorn forms natural hedges that are so impenetrable that they protect many birds that build their nests there. For this reason, the blackthorn has a high ecological value that must be respected. Before sprouting new leaves in spring, the blackthorn produces an intense flowering that, at a distance, makes it look like a totally white hedge formation. Its purplish-blue fruit, called "sloes," are used to make jams and liqueurs or to flavor gin or grappa. Reduced to a cream through boiling, the sloes were once used as an anti-diarrhoeic.

GLOSSARY

Akroterion
Architectural decorative element, often made of terracotta, that adorned the peak and two roof ends of sacred and public buildings or in tombs.

Aryballos
Greek term used to indicate a container for perfumed oils.

Bucchero
Type of Etruscan ceramics, black in color, obtained by means of a special firing process.

Calcarenite
Sedimentary rock formed by calcareous granules cemented by calcium carbonate.

Cinerary Urn
Vase destined to hold the bones or ashes of the dead after cremation.

Corbelled Dome
Vault formed by stone colonnades that jut out more as they rise and are then closed by horizontal slabs or an upside down wedge; it contrasts with the real dome in which the building device of thrust and counterthrust is closed by the keystone.

Crepidoma
Base.

Dromos
Entrance corridor.

Drum
Circular stone ring forming the base in several tumulus tomb typologies.

Eocene
A period of the Tertiary.

Etruscan-Corinthian
Defines the ceramics produced in several Etruscan centers in imitation of those produced in the city of Corinth in Greece.

Fibula
Stickpin made of bronze, silver or gold, used to fasten robes on the left shoulder; it is formed by the pin or tongue and the bow.

Galestro
Grayish-brown clayey schist.

Gorgoneion
Portrayal of the head of the Gorgon, or Medusa, monster of Greek mythology.

Hydria
Large vase for water with three handles: one vertical and two, smaller horizontal ones.

Hypogeum
Room built below ground level. An underground chamber tomb.

Kline (pl. Klinai)
Greek term meaning "bed," also used to indicate the dining couches used by the ancients.

Large Jar
A round vase used for cooking and preserving food.

Olocene
Final period of the Quaternary (the past 10,000 years).

Orientalizing
Phase of Etruscan civilization that occurred in the period between the last quarter of the VIII century and the early VI century BC, characterized by importing and imitating Oriental products and decorative motifs, destined to the ruling aristocratic classes.

Pediment
The front portion of a building covered by a double slanting roof and thus triangular.

Pendentive
Connecting structure between a square-plan room and a corbelled dome.

Pleistocene
Period of the Quaternary between 2 million and 10,000 years ago, at the time of the great glaciations.

Polis
Greek term used to indicate city-state.

Pronaos
From the Greek, the space between the cell of the temple and the columns standing before it.

Pyxis (pl. Pyxides)
Small cylindrical box with cover used to contain toilet articles.

Quaternary
The last geological era, characterized by great climatic insta-bility, with at least five glaciations, and strong variations of the sea level. It began some two million years ago.

Silt
Sediment containing a high percentage of lime (particles of a size ranging from sand to that of clay).

Tabula Peutingeriana
Medieval copy of a late-antiquity original (III-IV century AD) of a geographical map.

Villanovan
(culture) The name derives from Villanova, a locality in the area of Bologna where an Iron Age cremation necropolis (IX-VIII century BC) was found; used to indicate the civilization corresponding to this particular type of mortuary rite.

TO LEARN MORE

AA.VV., *Follonica etrusca. I segni di una civiltà*, pannelli della mostra, Follonica 1998

AA.VV., *L'Etruria Mineraria* (catalogo mostre), Milano 1985

CECCARELLI LEMUT M. L., GARZELLA G. (a cura di), *Populonia e Piombino in età medioevale e moderna*, atti del convegno, Ospedaletto (Pisa) 1996

CRISTOFANI M., *Gli Etruschi del mare*, Milano 1983

DENNIS G., *Itinerari etruschi da "The cities and cemeteries of Etruria"* a cura di M. Castagnola Roma 1976

FEDELI F., *Populonia. Storia e territorio*, Firenze 1983

FEDELI F., GALIBERTI A., ROMUALDI A., *Populonia e il suo territorio. Profilo storico-archeologico*, Firenze 1993

MINTO A., *Populonia,* Firenze 1943

ROMUALDI A., *Guida archeologica di Populonia*, Roma 1983

ROMUALDI A., *Una donna di rango a Populonia*, guida alla mostra, Firenze 1998

TORELLI M., *Storia degli Etruschi*, Bari 1981

Park System
of the Val di Cornia

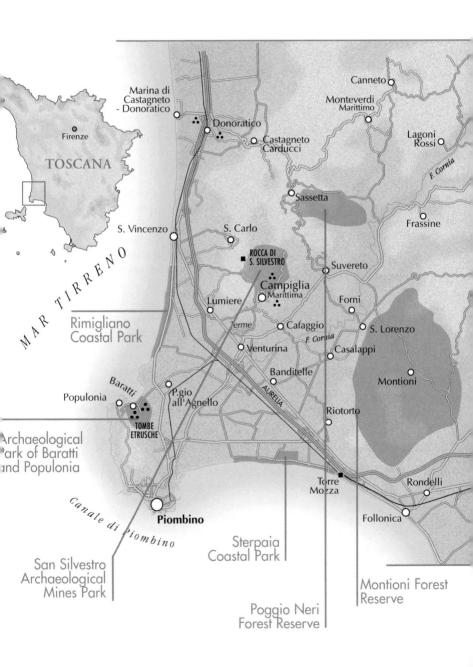

Canneto

Monteverdi
Marittimo

Lagoni
Rossi

Marina di
Castagneto
- Donoratico

Donoratico

Castagneto
Carducci

F. Cornia

TOSCANA

Firenze

Sassetta

Frassine

S. Vincenzo

S. Carlo

ROCCA DI
S. SILVESTRO

Suvereto

MAR TIRRENO

Campiglia
Marittima

Forni

Rimigliano
Coastal Park

Lumiere

Terme

Cafaggio

S. Lorenzo

F. Cornia

Casalappi

Venturina

Banditelle

Montioni

Baratti

Populonia

P.gio
all'Agnello

AURELIA

Riotorto

TOMBE
ETRUSCHE

Archaeological
Park of Baratti
and Populonia

Canale di Piombino

Piombino

Torre
Mozza

Rondelli

Follonica

San Silvestro
Archaeological
Mines Park

Sterpaia
Coastal Park

Montioni Forest
Reserve

Poggio Neri
Forest Reserve

Situated in west-central Tuscany, the Val di Cornia in the province of Livorno, is a territory that develops from the offshoots of the Metalliferous Hills to the coastal plain. Its total surface area of 365 square kilometers includes 6 natural and archaeological parks.
The Parks of the Val di Cornia were born in a territory with abundant historic emergences, hot springs, green forests, mineral deposits and kilometers of uncontaminated beaches. A natural and historic landscape where the signs of man's work become one with that of nature.

ARCHEOLOGICAL PARK
OF BARATTI AND POPULONIA
Piombino

From the slopes of the Piombino promontory and the Gulf of Baratti, the park spreads out for 80 hectares. It embraces a significant portion of the ancient Etruscan city with its necropolises, the calcarenite quarries and the industrial ironworking districts. Populonia, the only Etruscan city built on the sea, was one of the most important trade centers of the ancient world. The extreme importance of grave goods attests to the wealth of Populonian society, especially in relation to iron production and the strategic location of the port.
It is possible to retrace the signs of ironworking from the heaps of scoria visible on the beach to the "industrial" buildings. You can also visit one of the ancient calcarenite quarries, reused from the IV to the II centuries BC as a necropolis area where, by means of the signs left on the cutting surface, it is possible to reconstruct the stone extraction techniques.

STERPAIA
COASTAL PARK
Piombino

Located in the southern coastal area, it covers some 230 hectares. It is characterized by the presence of an important coastal wet forest with centuries-old oak trees, indicated as monumental trees. These are relics of the ancient original plain woods, typical of the plains inland of sand dunes which, in the past, were subjected to flooding and seasonal swamping. The trees (ash, manna ash and pubescent oak) thus originated spontaneously and can be seen in their natural aspect.

MONTIONI FOREST RESERVE
Suvereto, Piombino,
Campiglia
Marittima, Follonica

RIMIGLIANO
COASTAL PARK
San Vincenzo

POGGIO NERI
FOREST RESERVE
Sassetta

Situated between the Val di Cornia and the Val di Pecora, in the hills system between Massa Marittima and Suvereto, it spreads out for some 8000 hectares. These hills with their medium altitude are covered with woods that constitute a vegetal landscape closely tied to anthropic action. The history of Montioni is tied to carbon and wood-cutting. Indeed, since the XIX century, the forests of Montioni have represented a reservoir of carbon for the blast furnaces of Follonica and, for this reason, have undergone massive cutting. Another characteristic aspect is the presence of allume deposits (used for tanning hides and fixing colors on fabrics), widely exploited as of the XV century and, particularly, in the first decades of the XIX century, when prince and princess of Piombino, Felice and Elisa Baciocchi, founded a mining village (Montioni Nuovo), still visible today with its open-air and underground mines, forges and materials transportation system.

Located in the western coastal area, it spreads out for some 120 hectares. A prevalently natural park, though one can still sight several watchtowers of the coastal observation network, both Medieval and modern. The coastal dunes are well preserved with their pioneering vegetation and Mediterranean macchia inland. Part of the territory was formerly a lake (lake Rimigliano), dried between the mid XIX and the first decades of the XX century. In addition to vegetational aspects, there is interesting evidence that refers to the study of the ancient swamp areas and coastal lakes of the Cornia plain.

Located in the hilly area in the vicinity of Sassetta, it spreads out for some 700 hectares, 600 of which are entirely covered by woods. Along with its enormous vegetational and faunal interest, it presents the typical features of the hilly woods of Maremma, with a strong presence of ungulates in the free state.

SAN SILVESTRO ARCHAEO-LOGICAL MINES PARK
Campiglia Marittima

The Park, situated within the hills of the mountain range of Campiglia Marittima, extends for some 450 hectares. These medium-high hills are characterized by the presence of rich mining deposits of copper, lead, silver and zinc. From the proto-historic period until the seventies, the extraction and working of these metals was the territory's main activity. The traces left by Etruscan, Medieval, Renaissance and modern mining and metallurgical processes, lead the visitor to understand the ancient extraction techniques and the history of this mining territory. Among mining settlements, the medieval castle of Rocca San Silvestro is particularly interesting and was founded by the Gherardesca counts on the threshold of the year one thousand. The particular state of conservation of the settlement and its early abandonment, in the course of the XIV century, make it one of the most interesting examples to understand the life, economy and material culture of medieval Tuscany. A portion of the mining system (the tunnel of Temperino) has been opened to the public and constitutes a suggestive subterranean visit in search of ancient and modern cavities created by mining. **With the PARCHI PASS initiative, visitors to the Archaeological Park of Baratti and Populonia are entitled to a 50% discount on ticket price for the full visit to the San Silvestro Archeological Mines Park.**

The medieval village of Rocca San Silvestro (X-XIV centuries AD).

below:
The learning workshop of the San Silvestro Archaeological Mines Park.

Infoparchi

Parchi Val di Cornia S.p.A.
Via Lerario 90, 57025 Piombino (Li)
Tel. 0565/49430 Fax 0565/49733
Email HYPERLINK mailto:parchi.valdicornia@parchivaldicornia.it

San Silvestro Archaeological Mines Park
Via di San Vincenzo 34b, Campiglia M.ma (Li)
Tel. 0565/838680 Fax 0565/838703,
Email HYPERLINK mailto:parcoss@parchivaldicornia.it

Archaeological Park of Baratti e Populonia
Loc. Baratti, 57025 Piombino (Li)
Tel. 0565/29002 Fax 0565/29107
Email HYPERLINK mailto:parcobp@parchivaldicornia.it

The many historic and natural emergences of this territory have made it possible to plan various itineraries and elaborate visiting proposals to the Val di Cornia Parks, lasting not only one day, but even two or more days.

The programs we propose to groups of students and adults combine guided visits to museums, archaeological sites and historic centers, interesting outdoor workshops and moments of enogastronomy where they can taste typical local products.

For detailed information on programs, call or fax the Archaeological Park offices and speak to Carla Casalini or Chiara Cilli (Tel. 0565/838680 - 0567/29002).
Proposals can be partially modified and personalized.

Instructions for Use

Getting There *Road links:* On the Livorno-Roma motorway proceeding north, take one of the San Vincenzo Nord exits, or the Venturina exit if you are arriving from the south.
Trains: Populonia Scalo station (Tel. 055.225263) on the Campiglia Marittima-Piombino secondary line.
Campiglia Marittima station (0565.851476) on the Livorno-Roma line.
Bus Service: Buses from San Vincenzo, Piombino, Campiglia Marittima and Populonia Scalo are provided by ATM.
Tel. 0564.260111 – 0565.260184.

Sea and Beaches The Archaeological Park of Baratti and Populonia is located very near one of the finest beaches of Tuscany. The Gulf of Baratti, a crescent moon between the tip of Populonia Alta and the promontory of Villa del Barone, is the perfect setting to spend days at the sea.

Prices Admissions tickets to the Archaeological Park are priced according to the itinerary chosen. Reductions are offered to groups, age categories and families. The combined ticket is valid for one week, and all tickets issued at the Archaeological Park of Baratti entitle the bearer to a 50% reduction on entrance to the nearby San Silvestro Archaeological Mines Park. Residents can purchase season tickets at the park entrance.

Hours In summer months (July and August), the Park is open every day from 9 am until 8 pm. In June and September, the Park observes the same hours, but closes on Monday. In March, April, May and October, the Park is open every day, except Monday, from 9 am until sunset. In autumn and winter (November-February), the Park is open Saturday and Sunday from 10 am until 5 pm and on weekdays from 9 am until 2 pm. Closed Monday.

Guided Tours During opening hours, throughout the year, several guided tours (booking required in winter) are conducted to the necropolis of San Cerbone and to the Necropolises of Le Grotte along the Via delle Cave. Visits can also be conducted in English, French and German.

Parking The Park disposes of a vast tended parking facility, free of charge for visitors to the archaeological area. Pay parking facilities for campers and caravans to spend the night are also available and offer the possibility to drain waste waters and replenish drinking water.

Bathroom Facilities Inside the Park, two fully equipped rest areas provide bathroom facilities, a refreshment stand, bookshop, souvenir sales outlet.

Index

Printed in Florence
at the printing-house of Edizioni Polistampa
May 2002